HISTORICAL AND GENEALOGICAL RECORD OF THE VILLANUEVA BROTHERS

VICENTE VILLANUEVA AND MARIANO PORFERIO VILLANUEVA

With

Annotated Genealogical Summary of the Villanueva Family

Abridged Version

Compiled By

Angela Villanueva Rios – Howe

Copyright © 2019 by Angela Villanueva Rios - Howe

ALL RIGHTS RESERVED. Written permission must be secured from the author to use or reproduce any part of this book, in any form or by any means, including electronic reproduction, except for brief quotations in critical reviews or articles.

Published by

Janaway Publishing, Inc.
732 Kelsey Ct.
Santa Maria, California 93454
(805) 925-1038
www.JanawayPublishing.com

2019

ISBN: 978-1-59641-431-0 (Paperback)

ISBN: 978-1-59641-432-7 (Hardbound)

This work is an abridged version of the historical and genealogical record of the Villanueva Brothers, Vicente Villanueva and Mariano P. Villanueva, with an annotated genealogical summary of the Villanueva family, compiled by Angela Villanueva Rios-Howe. Janaway Publishing, Inc., the publisher of this work, does not give or make any representation or warranty (either express or implied) as to the completeness, accuracy or reliability of the contents of this work.

Made in the United States of America

To all my relatives who wish to know about the saga of the Villanueva family.

Table of Contents

Abridge Version: *Historical And Genealogical Record Of The Villanueva Brothers, Vicente Villanueva and Mariano Porferio Villanueva*

Note_____vii

Acknowledgment_____xi-xii

Introduction_____xiii-xxxii

Chapter I

Vicente Villanueva (I) and His Family; Genealogical Chart------------------------------1-5

Chapter II

Mariano P. Villanueva (I) and His Family; Genealogical Chart-----------------------6-42

Chapter III

Annotated Genealogical Summary of the Villanueva Family-----------------------------43-126

Chapter IV

List of Villanueva Families by Generation---127-141

Note

I find it very difficult to write about one's own family history. I wish somebody else would do it. Our ancestors' downfall is a very sad and a tragic one and no matter how you look at it, it will have a profound effect on everyone.

After listening to opinions and suggestions regarding the rough draft of this genealogical record, I made considerable changes in my method of writing, however, I did my best not to alter or to modify the contributed materials as suggested by some relatives. I am very much aware that by preserving some of the claims and original statements made by relatives through telephone and taped interviews here and abroad; conversation during casual meetings or at parties; and through e-mails and letters would cause some grief or resentments from surviving relatives.

Writing a "cleaned up and modified" genealogical history with favorable wording and sequence of events so to avoid offending and hurting the feelings of living relatives would be leading them farther away from the truth and the realities of the true lives of our ancestors; how they had lived; perceived the world and treated other people.

I really do not mind being embarrassed; subjected to redicule and poked fun at but sometimes I cannot avoid feeling frustrated when my inquiries and request for information are often ignored. Also, I had been accused multiple times of being gullible. Many people had doubted the accuracy of the information that I had gathered regarding the Villanueva family. I do not blame them for I do not have a way of verifying the truthfulness and authenticity of some of the information given and quoted here and could go no further back in time to search for any data to crosscheck and authenticate the contributed materials. The best thing that I could do is to carefully annotate the contributed materials.

It is a fact, that there will always be relatives with differing and conflicting perception and recollection of events. But the more relatives contribute; regardless whether their ideas are different or the same as the others, the more we will have materials to consider and to base our opinions regarding the matter.

My sole intention and purpose of doing this genealogy is to preserve the history of our family. It is not my intention to hurt, insult or belittle and or exclude anyone. If you have the chance to read this genealogical history, kindly excuse whatever you think had been omitted and whatever you deemed to be erroneous presentation of people and events. Before you make judgment on any of the actions and behaviors of our relatives, dead or alive, please remember the circumstances and society they were in at that very moment. We must learn to accept the fact that our ancestors, like anybody else, had shortcomings, prejudices and weaknesses.

As their stories unfold, we can take time to contemplate our own lives and see if our attitudes and values are any better than them.

Historical And Genealogical Record Of The Villanueva Brothers

Vicente Villanueva and Mariano Porferio Villanueva Sr.

With Annotated Genealogical Summary of the Villanueva Family

Abridged Version

Acknowledgment

I give my sincere appreciation to all my relatives who have contributed to this compilation and most of all to our mother, Angela Villanueva Villanueva Rios Sr. (I), who accommodated me when I interviewed her about her family. It must have been very painful for her to reflect on the past.

Many thanks to my siblings, Ate Pat (Patricia Wood); Carlos Manuel; Maria Teresa Concepcion and her husband, Dr.Resurrection Gregorio Kare; Jaime Miguel and Amelia Fragante Rios who were generous enough to give me the diplomas and pictures of Mama; Andres, who connected me to relatives that he often socialized with; and to Cesar Antonio whose suggestions, as far as writing style is concerned and editing were greatly appreciated. Although, I am surprised by Antonio's regards of the past as irrelevant and does not want to look back, his love for documentaries and for old historical books is surprisingly remarkable and conflicting.

Many thanks and appreciation to: our Aunt, Consuelo Villanueva Torres Jr. (II); to our cousins, Antonio Morales Villanueva; Rafael Cope Villanueva; to Marichu Crisol Reynolds; Muriel de Lejos Riosa, Orestes Murillo Morales, and his wife, Dolores Dy Alparce Morales; Margarita de Lejos Buenconsejo, who had given me relevant information, especially dates, regarding the Villanueva family; to Mely Madrid Lopez, a cousin in Canada, for giving me clarification regarding Luis Madrid and to her husband, Jesus, who had helped me with some of the translations; to our nieces, Edna Buenconsejo Lao, who helped interview Eta (Margarita Buenconsejo) regarding her memories of the family. Edna was also instrumental in procuring old pictures and documents of our grandparents, Pedro and Quiteria Villanueva and other relatives, finding the right names of Mariano Porfirio Villanueva and Antonio Villanueva, and documents from the Philippine National Archives; to Grace Pleta Herrera; to Anita Buenconsejo Bonganay; to Annie Riosa Nañoz; to our nephews, Robert Lianco who had gone out of his way to help me track down relatives and take pictures of tombstones; to Edbert V. Albarico; Chito V. Guinto; Delia Guinto Santiago; Hector Awitin Morales Jr. (III); to our grand niece Hani, (Corina Belle Riosa Villar) who had given me websites and links to the Internet and old pictures of relatives and Tabaqueños; and to Vicki Antipolo of Singapore.

I can never thank enough Mike Farris for his unending help he had extended me. He is the IT person of Santa Maria Valley Historical SocietyMuseum who had been helping me with my computer; he had helped me navigate Microsoft Words; giving me ideas and suggestions regarding how to do genealogical work.

I give my thanks to Cindy Ransick, the Curator of Santa Maria Valley Historical Society Museum, Santa Maria, California, in helping me with the handheld scanner, giving me information about local publisher and for being patient while I distract Mike from his Museum work with my questions.

To all other relatives and friends, that I had failed to mention here but just as important, you have my gratitude.

As I said in my other work "*Guirómduma Mán Tábi*", I have to thank Cherry Malquiades of the Philippine National Library for sending me the documents regarding the towns and barrios of Albay. It is from these collections of documents that I was able to get most of the information regarding *Batan Islands*. My thanks to Rosalyn Pachoaca, Reference Librarian, Newspaper & Current Periodicals Room, Serial & Government Publication Division of Library of Congress, for her help with the October 21, 1896 publication of "El Comercio" newspaper.

I also would like to thank Dr. Norman Owen for giving me information regarding links to more information about the Villanuevas. I am grateful to all authors whose work I had used in this genealogy.

To Honorable Victorino Mapa Manalo, Executive Director of the Philippine National Archives, and his staff, I give my sincere thanks for sending me documents regarding Bicol and about the Villanuevas of the Bicol Region through Edna Lao.

I thank and appreciate my husband and my children, who had put up with all the paper mess and my inattention to household chores. I want to give my special thanks to Chris and Jeoffrey for helping me with my iMack problems and to Jonathan for teaching me how to save and transfer pictures and with all other computer problems.

I do not have the time to include the details of the 4th generation in this abridged copy. I will leave that to other younger relatives who have the time and energy to do it.

Angela Villanueva Rios Howe

California 2019

Introduction

Most of the information regarding the family of Vicente Villanueva and his brother Mariano Porferio Villanueva Sr. (I) as well as Pedro Arana Villanueva Sr. (I) and Quiteria Mabihis Villanueva (I) is based on my actual recorded interview with our mother, Angela Villanueva Villanueva Rios Sr. (I), who was the youngest daughter of Pedro Arana Villanueva (I) and Quiteria Mabihis Villaneuva (I), and granddaughter of both Vicente Villanueva (I) and Mariano P. Villanueva (I).

The telephone interviews with Muriel de Lejos Riosa (I) and her sister, Margarita de Lejos Buenconsejo (I), who both grew up with their younger siblings under the roof of their grandmother, Quiteria, gave a lot of insight as to the habit and lifestyle in the household of the Villanuevas.

Our family history can only go as far back to Vicente (I) and Mariano Porferio Villanueva (I), known in some history books as the *"Villanueva Brothers"*[1]. Our mother, Angela Sr. (I), the granddaughter of both men, said that "they went to Bicol from Iloilo, and started a hemp (*sinamay, and rope making*) business.[2] Their Company was called Messrs. Villanueva & Co.[3]

There are several claims as to where Vicente (I) and Mariano P. (I) originated. As Angela Sr. (I) had claimed, they were from Iloilo but according to Orestes Morales (I), Fermin Ante Villanueva (I), a grandson of Mariano P.Villanueva (I), and the oldest son of Delfin Arana Villanueva (I), "several Villanueva brothers came from Barcelona and upon reaching the Philippines, separated, and went to different parts of the country. Some went to the northern part of the Philippines and some settled in the south."[4]

Another grand-daughter of Mariano P. (I), the youngest daughter of Mariano Villanueva (II), Consuelo Bautista Villanueva Torres (II), also claimed that, "Vicente (I) and Mariano P. (I) were Spaniards from Barcelona."[5]

However, Dr. Norman Owen in his book, **The Bikol Blend** : *Bikolanos and Their History* wrote that the Villanueva brothers were *"Manila born Chinese Mestizos"*.[6]

Angela (I), until her death in 1992, never wavered in her claim as to where her grandfathers came from - Iloilo where there are Villanuevas still living to this day.

The Barcelona origin cannot be verified. Dr. Owen cited *"Protocoles de Albay"* as his source of his information.

The latest information that had been received on May 7, 2019 from Chito Villanueva Guinto through Delia Guinto Santiago of Naga, Camarines Sur, that Dr. Vicente Villanueva (III) was initially buried at the Tabaco Chinese Cemetery before his remains was transferred to Pili, seems to support Dr. Owen's Chinese lineage claim but their origin is still in question.

Several plausible assumptions based on this information can be made concerning the Villanueva brothers' place of origin:

a. that the father (of Vicente and Mariano) and his brothers were most likely the ones who originally came from Barcelona. They settled in the commercial centers of the country, which, at that time were Manila, Ilocos, and Iloilo where they intermarried with Chinese, Filipinos and other ethnic groups.

b. it is most probable that, although Vicente's and Mariano's parents main residence was in Iloilo, they likely maintained another house in Manila where the two brothers were born because of the existence of good hospitals in the capital. It is not uncommon for rich families to maintain several houses in different locations.

c. the Villanueva brothers probably studied in Manila and were later sent to Barcelona to further their studies.

At the time, it was the custom of prominent Filipino families, the so-called *ilustrados* to send their sons abroad to study. Most Filipinos went to Spain, - Spain being considered the mother country. Other favorite destinations of rich young men were Hong-Kong, London, and Germany. However, most of them went to Madrid and Barcelona.

d. Probably, when the Villanueva brothers finished their studies abroad and came home, they decided to start their own business in Albay province.

The two brothers took advantage of the booming abaca industry and went to Albay just like what Dr. Norman Owen had written, " ...*with many others from "Manila, and Tagalog regions" and which included the "seven of the fifteen "Bikol Martyrs" migrated to Bicol to take advantage of the boom in the abaca industry."* [7]

The profitability of the cultivation of abaca brought many other entrepreneurs from other places. Among the people from Iloilo are the "*Locsin, Los Baños, Baylon and Jaucian*"[8] whose descendants can still be found in Legaspi. While the descendants of *Madrid* and *Villanueva*, who are related, can be found both in Naga, Legaspi and in Tabaco. Many had moved to Manila and migrated abroad.

Vicente Villanueva (I) settled in Legaspi and Mariano P. Villanueva (I) settled in Tabaco but they remained business partners till the death of Vicente (I) in 1891 (?).[9]

It would be safe to say that the Villanueva brothers were from a rich family because they can afford to put up a business of producing Sinamay and Abaca cordage, which require substantial amount of capital.

During the Spanish rule in the 1800, it was not easy and not everybody could establish a Hemp business more so a plantation of Abaca anywhere in the Philippines.

The difficulties in establishing this kind of business venture was not only due to limited availability of land in areas conducive to growing Abaca; owning lands by foreigners who are the most in the position to have the capital to invest, was restricted. This restriction helped lessen the competition.

Mr. Alex Gollan, the British Consuls that served in Manila in 1891, reported on the restrictions in owning land by foreigners in the Philippines which were, at the time, strictly enforced. He prepared a report titled, **"Report on Hemp Cultivation in the Philippine Islands"** in February 14, 1891 for Sir James Ferguson. The report was addressed to the Marquis of Salisbury. Though this report was prepared in the year Vicente Villanueva died and the later years of the lives of the Villanueva brothers, it best summed up the difficulties of establishing, owning or purchasing lands for the cultivation of Abaca (Musa Textiles or so called Manila Hemp) in the Philippine islands in the late 19th Century.

> *"The cost of preparing and planting a quiñon (about 7 acres), and keeping it clean up to the time of the first crop, is estimated at from 200 dol. to 300 dol., not including the first cost of the land; and afterwards an annual outlay of about 60 dol. would be required to keep the soil free from weeds, &c. The extent of land mentioned, after the plantation is three years old, would produce from 16 bales to 20 bales of hemp per annum, according to the quality of the soil.*
>
> *It is most difficult to give an accurate estimate of the first cost of land suitable for hemp production. The best places are, of course, already taken up, and intending purchases would now have to content themselves with uncultivated and uncleared lands mainly in the islands of Mindanao, Samar, Leyte and Negros. Such uncultivated tracts might perhaps be obtained from the Spanish Government at an average price of 1 dol. per acre, but proximity to a shipping port would enhance the value considerably. As regards to the purchase of estates already cleared and in working order it is quite impossible to give even an approximate, as the industry being a very profitable one to those who understand it an occupier would not be likely to part with his property except at a fancy price. I need scarcely say that almost, without exception, landowners who devote themselves to the production of hemp are European Spaniards or natives of these islands, and a foreigner would have considerable difficulty in establishing himself, and would meet with many obstacles before he found himself in touch with his surroundings. The language - I do not here speak of Spanish, but of the different dialects of Malay - would in itself be an important obstacle at the onset, and there are drawbacks, such as a trying Climate, the nature and disposition of the native labourer, the isolated and semi-civilized kind of life a man would have to lead to ensure success, and others of a like nature which a foreigner would do well to ponder over before embarking his capital in such venture."*[10]

It not only takes an average of three years to have a full crop harvest, the plant needs a lot of moisture and is easily destroyed by strong winds or typhoon which is prevalent in the Bicol Region.

Abaca was popularly called Manila hemp although the plant is not grown in that area. It may be due to the fact that during the Spanish rule, the Abaca produced by most provinces were sent to Manila before export. In the yearly British Reports on Trade and Commerce of the Philippine Islands, hemp production and exports were usually recorded under the heading of Hemp from Manila, Cebu and Iloilo. In fact, it was only in the British report dated 1900 of the Acting British Consul Sinclair that hemp produced in Albay and Sorsogon were mentioned.

Vicente (I) and Mariano (I) created the Messrs. Villanueva & Co. with Mariano (I) owning half and managing the company alone. Among the assets of the company was "a cargo boat",[11] which was also "used as passenger boat for vacationing Villanuevas from Manila."[12] They also "owned one of the two piers in the town of Tabaco."[13]

The pier that they owned could be accessed through the road now called Bonifacio St. where the main house of Mariano (I) and the house of one of his sons, Mariano (II), lay alongside his. His son's house was later sold and used as a "trade school named, Fisheries High School."[14] Mariano's (I) house was later sold to Smith Bell and Co. Then acquired by Angela Manalang Gloria.[15]

The other pier parallel to the Villanueva's and can be accessed through the road near the Tabaco municipal building was owned by the rich Don Mariano Riosa's (I) family whose son, Santiago (I), later married Francisca Arana Villanueva, the daughter of Mariano P. Villanueva.

The interesting love story of Francisca Villanueva (I), to Don Santiago Riosa (I) led to the "joining of the two piers making it a horseshoe shaped structure."[16] Whether the joining of the two piers was due to this union is open to speculation.

There is no given description and dimension of the cargo boat owned by the Merrs. Villanueva & Company, though it can safely be surmised that it was big because it "was used for the transportation of hemp, copra and passengers."[17] There is no record or recollection of the boat being used for the coal that they mined in Batan Island where they owned several *pertenencias* or holdings of the "first class kind"[18], or "gold from their holdings in a gold mine."[19]

This "*goleta*" as it is called back then or sailboat, may be just as big and similar to the "*goletas*" described by Nora Villanueva Daza in her cookbook , *"Festive Dishes,"* owned by her ancestors - Gregorio Villanueva, which "*were used to transport goods and people throughout the country. That's why there are Villanuevas in Bicol and in Iloilo*".[20]

The extent of the Villanueva's involvement in coal mining, especially in Batan Island, had been described in the report to the U.S. Military Governor in the Philippines in 1901 by Charles H. Burritt, First Lieutenant, Eleventh Cavalry, U.S.V., and Officer in Charge the Mining Bureau.

Batan Island, according to First Lieutenant Burritt, had been mined since 1847 under the governorship of Velarde but the coal mining industry in the Philippine Island was never really developed to its full potential under the Spanish rule. It is believed that the entire Batan Island is made of coal of good quality.

According to **The Coal Measures Of The Philippines**, Chapter XXI, - The Island of Batan: by First Lieutenant Charles H. Burritt:[21]

"In 1893 location of coal in Batan Island was located.

"By reference to the table for the last half of the period covered by this report it will be observed that locations of coal were made in the year 1893 on the Island of Batan, and almost simultaneously by three different parties-the "Sodupe," by Gil Brothers, consisting of two pertenencias2 on the 20th of December; the "Balerma," "Urgera," and "Granalda," of one pertenencia each, on 21th of December of the same year, by Messrs. Villanueva & Co; and the "San Francisco," of four pertenencias, by Emilio Muñoz, on the 30th of December 1893.

In the year 1894 there was added to the Gil Brothers group of mines the "Bilbao," of four pertenencias; the "Lucas y Josefa," of one pertenencia, and the "Chitfladura," also of one pertenencia; and to the properties of Messrs. Villanueva & Co., the "Perseverancia," of one pertenencia. In March 1895, Gil Brothers presented petitions for the "Presentancion" and the Olaveaga," of two pertenencias each. All of the above-named mines were conceded, and titled issued by the Spanish Government in the latter part of the year1895, which is all of the mines on the island of Batan of the "first class;" that is, those for which concessions had been issued by the Spanish Government prior to the American occupation. This makes twelve pertennecias in the Gil Brothers group, and four each in those of Messrs. Villanueva & Co. and Emilio Muñoz."

The report included the results of the first assay of the coal found in Batan Island. The first assay of the coal sample was made in Madrid in the year 1853.

Frederic H. Sawyer, however, in his book *"The Inhabitants of the Philippine Island"*, written in 1900 disputed the quality of the coal found in the Philippines.[22]

"It is common to see coal mentioned amongst the mineral resources of the Philippines, but so far as I have been able to learn, no true coal has been found here, nor in any adjacent islands. There are beds of lignite of varying qualities..."

Mr. Sawyer's claim had been supported by the findings of Professor George W. Becker of the United States Geological Survey. At the request of Admiral Dewey, Professor Becker prepared a memorandum, which was forwarded to the Navy Department. He stated that:

"The coal… can be best characterized as highly carbonized lignite, likely to contain much Sulphur as iron pyrites, rendering them apt to spontaneous combustion and injurious to boilers plates. Nevertheless…when pyrites seams are avoided and the lignite is properly handled, it forms a valuable fuel, especially for local consumption."[23]

In 1952-53, the President of the Philippines required the Bureau of Public Schools to collect historical, cultural and traditional data of all the towns and barrios of the Philippines. Although the printed copies made from the microfilm of the data collected under the heading "Barrio of Batan", which was formerly known as the *"visita of Anonang"*[24], are in very poor condition, some data were legible enough to get more information.

Fig.1. Satellite image from Map data Google 2018 [25]

The report mentioned the coal mining activity in the area during the Spanish time up to the Japanese occupation. The accuracy of the report needed verification.

According to the report, a certain *"Don Pascual Villanueva (?)"*, instead of Mariano (I) Villanueva, *"headed the private coal mining company in Batan, which was later discontinued"*.[26] The most probable reason for the interruption of working the mines could be due to the Filipino – American War as mentioned in the report by a British Consul.

The British report on Trade in the Philippines, mentioned that during the rebellion of the Filipinos against the Americans, the mining and the hemp industries suffered momentarily because some were abandoned due to lack of laborers.

There are very few available data regarding the mines in Batan Island during the war and during the American occupation. However, in this particular report collected and submitted by the Public School Teachers as required by the Bureau of Public School in 1952-53 stated (without citing the source of the information): [27]

4th paragraph:

"In 1902 (?) -1904, a certain private company called "East Batan Company" under the management of Mr. Arlington Betts (?) operated again the mines of Batan which was discontinued by the private company headed by Don Pascual (?)Villanueva."

6th paragraph:

"Later on this company was bankrupt. The operation was stayed. Then in 1917-"1920" (?), the Philippine coal Mine continued the operation under the management of Mr. Jack Barker. The same improvement was made for the barrio. Again this company was bankrupt. The operation was continued by Don Vicente Villanueva and was caught by the war.

During the Japanese Occupation, the Coal Mines were restored by Don Vicente Villanueva under the management of the late Juan "Ramos" (?) but controlled by the Japanese."

The report further stated that after the liberation, the operation of the mines continued. The rest of the information was illegible.

The accuracy of this report could not be confirmed since most of them were done by interviewing people who may have had knowledge or memories of the past and not necessarily based on available factual written evidence.

No record of a Pascual (?) Villanueva was ever mentioned by surviving relatives of Mariano (I) and Vicente (I) to have headed the Messrs. Villanueva & Co. The question arises whether Vicente (I) or Mariano (I) have a relative named Pascual? There was a Mayor of Pasay whose name was Pascual Villanueva. Could the person interviewed by the teacher in the Bureau of Public School Report mean "Pedro Villanueva (I)", the oldest son of Mariano (I) and Teodora Arana?

Don Vicente Villanueva (I), that was also later mentioned in the Bureau of Public School Report, to have re-established the Batan coal mine operation after Mr. Jack Barker, could not be the brother of Mariano (I), since Vicente (I) died in 1891 as reported by Dr. Norman G. Owen and all the holdings of the Msrrs Villanueva & Co.'s holdings in Batan Coal Mines were only registered in 1896. He could very well be the son of Mariano P.Villanueva (I) - Vicente A. Villanueva (II).

Note: *The use of the Roman numerals after each name is used for genealogical clarification only.*

It was probably Vicente (II) or Pedro Sr. (I) who has had a hand in managing the business of the Messrs. Villanueva & Co., and administering the share of his first cousins, particularly the inheritance of Quiteria the only surviving daughter of Vicente Villanueva (I)] before it was entirely disposed of by Mariano P. (I).

Quiteria M.Villanueva (I) was the oldest daughter of Vicente Villanueva (I). When she inherited her share of her father's holdings, Mariano P. (I) became the administrator of her entire estate. Quiteria's (I) youngest daughter, Angela (I) said, "Mariano P. (I) never gave Quiteria (I) her inheritance especially her shares of the "Minas de Batan" after he sold it. Mariano P. (I) sold the Batan Island Coal Mine holdings to deliberately deprive Quiteria (I) of her inheritance." [28]

Although this action of Mariano (I) is consistent with his reputation as seemingly "unprincipled" individual, in his defense, we can cite that by the time Messrs Villanueva & Company had holdings at a coal mine in Batan (1895), Vicente (I) had been dead for four years (as Dr. Owen had mentioned that he died in 1891) It appears that Mariano P. (I) was still solely responsible for running the company and the partnership appears to be still intact. In all legality Quiteria (I) was entitled to her share as heir of Vicente (I). It is understandable for Mariano P. (I) to harbor "resentment" for sharing the bounty of the company that he had expanded with someone who had no hand in running the company.

With regards to the running of the coal mine in Batan after the Filipino-American War, the only other Vicente in the family would be the grandson – Dr. Vicente Villanueva Villanueva (III) who is unlikely to be the one mentioned in the Batan Report.

Vicente (III), the grandson, was the oldest son of Pedro Sr. (I) and Quiteria Villanueva (I). He would still be in school studying in Santo Tomas University School of Medicine rather than managing the Coal Mines in Batan Island. Angela (I), the youngest sister of Vicente (III), who had been the source of most of the information about the Villanueva family, never mentioned him managing the business or the mines. Vicente (III) practiced medicine in Tabaco where he died of cerebral hemorrhage on July 24, 1933.[29]

Pedro Sr. (I), the oldest son of Mariano P. (I) and the husband of Quiteria most likely helped in managing the business being the oldest. Jaime Miguel V. Rios (I), the grandchild of Pedro Sr. (I) and Quiteria (I); (Angela's (I) 7th child) with Jesus Salvador B. Rios (I), visited and researched the Rapu-Rapu islands to find if there are still properties owned by the Villanuevas in that island. Jaime Miguel (I) said that Pedro Sr. (I), "was still mentioned as the owner of some properties in Rapu-Rapu, and land tax is still paid in his behalf ."[30] Rapu-Rapu is in proximity to Batan Island.

The Villanueva brothers lived luxurious lives. Vicente (I) lived in Legaspi and was said that his furniture, particularly, the dining table and chairs were encrusted with gold and semi – precious stones. Angela (I) said that, "his wife, Tomas, took all pieces of furniture back to Spain when he died. The house was inherited by Quiteria."[31]

According to Dr. Norman Goodner Owen (1984, Owen, p. 214), "It is true that at the pinnacle of the economic structure a new "super elite" emerged, composed of affluent outsiders and Bikolanos whose, property, power and education were far in excess of those of ordinary *principales.* There is no equivalent at the beginning of the nineteenth century to the Spanish owned "Causip" hacienda or the estate of the Tagalog-Chinese mestizo merchant Vicente Villanueva (valued at over P200,000) at the end…"[32]

Mariano P. (I) had two big houses in Tabaco and both brothers, maintained houses not only in Legaspi, and in Tabaco but also in Malate. Their children, particularly the sons also owned several houses in Tabaco, in Albay in Legaspi, and in Alhambra in Malate.

Mariano P. (I) 's reputation as an alleged "land grabber" Villanueva" (1984, Owen, p. 87) and womanizer was legend.

Dr. Owen stated, "…one instance of substantial usurpation of communal and private lands was alleged around the turn of the century. The Tagalog-Chinese mestizo Mariano P. Villanueva, one of the major abaca traders of the region, was accused of "grabbing" over 1,000 hectares of communal grazing lands, perhaps including some small unregistered farms, on the island of San Miguel, opposite the town of Tabaco. The allegation is not proven (in the available evidence), but it is consonant with the kinds of abuses that often occurred elsewhere in the Philippines…"[33]

The aforementioned accusation of so called " land grabbing" of Mariano P. (I) was litigated by the Philippine Supreme Court on October 10, 1913: *.G.R. No. L-7309, October 10, 1913MIGUEL BERSES and 318 others, plaintiff-appellants, vs. MARIANO P. VILLANUEVA, defendant-appellee. Singson, Ledesma and Lim, and Tirso de Irureta Goyena for appellants.Manly and McMahon for appellee.]*[34]

The court sided with Mariano P. Villanueva (I) as the true owner of the land in question.

According to some people of the town of Tabaco, he made philandering fashionable. Fermin Ante Villanueva (I), told Orestes Villanueva Morales (I), that, "Mariano P. (I) went about his business in a carriage driven by a servant and drawn by three pairs of horses. Whenever he sees a pretty lady, he would tell his servant to investigate where she lives and gather information about the woman. Mariano would later go to the house of the woman - carrying with him a land title as a bribe for her to have extramarital relationship with him."[35]

Having cocktails after coming home from work and having imported food, wine, silk clothing, and other personal accessories from Europe was a common preference for the family.[36]

Spanish was predominantly spoken at home especially among the family members. English, Tagalog and Bicol were spoken as well.

The children of both Vicente (I) and Mariano P. (I), especially the sons were sent either to Hong-Kong or Europe to study and the girls who were given music and singing lessons by private tutors - were sent to convents and finishing schools in Manila to study.[37]

Most of the grandchildren went to Alhambra Primary School. In high school, the granddaughters were sent as "*internas*" to Colegio Centro Escolar de Señoritas, which was, according to Dr. Alip, "was one of the most outstanding private Universities in Manila." [38]

Colegio Centro Escolar de Señoritas exclusive school for girls was established on June 3, 1907 by Librada Avelino and Carmen de Luna. One or both of them was related to the Villanueva and considered very close to the family. The school hired a lot of Villanueva relatives, some of whom lived at the dormitory of the school until they died. The school is now known as Centro Escolar University, which, later in the 1970's, became a coed University offering 4-5 years courses in different academic fields.

In 1887, during the Exposicion General de Las Islas Filipinas in Madrid, Vicente (I) and Mariano P. (I) contributed and gave items to be exhibited. They were among the many Bicolanos who were exhibitors in the "1887 Exposicion".in Madrid.[39]

According to Dr. Owens, *Bikol Blend*, when Vicente died, "was worth P200,000.00 pesos and when Mariano died, he was worth P400,000.00.29 pesos." [40]

No one really knew the real worth of Mariano P. (I) and Vicente (I) when they died, according to their granddaughter, Angela Villanueva Rios (I). The pieces of furniture encrusted with gold and semi precious stones of Vicente (I), which were taken back to Spain by his wife and son, Tomas and Balbino; the gold coins collection of Mariano (I), which were rumored he had thrown at sea between San Miguel Island and Tabaco pier and also rumored to have been inherited by Isidora Arana Villanueva were invaluable.

During their lifetime, the Villanueva brothers and some of their children gave the town of Tabaco unparalleled bequest. Orestes Morales (I) said that, " these include the land for Tabaco Municipal Building,[41] and "a big bell for the bell tower of the church of Tabaco."[42]

Pedro Sr. (I) and Quiteria Villanueva (I) donated "7 hectares of land for the establishment of what is now called the Tabaco National High School situated in the barrio of Panal but the town of Tabaco took more than 7 hectares and it is said that there was no existing deed. " [43] Part of the Villanueva property was made into a road that leads to the barrios of Guinobat and Mariroc. Although they did not officially donate the strip of land for the road or the land alongside the river, the town officials assumed that those track of land belonged to the government. [44]

Fig. 2. Mrs. Angela Villanueva Rios receiving the plaque of appreciation in behalf of the Villanueva heirs in April 1969 at Tabaco High School Commencement Exercise.

Fig. 3. Certificate of Appreciation to the Villanueva Heirs presented by the Tabaco High School PTA and the Tabaco High School Administration in April, 1969.

The pier is now a public domain and remained in use to this day for local and international shipping but the bell which is said to be still in the bell tower suffered a big crack and was never repaired by the Catholic Church of Tabaco.[45]

The ancestral home of Mariano P. (I) was sold to Smith Bell & Co., which was later sold to Angela Manalang Gloria and later converted to a Museum. All the other "big houses were sold and became high school buildings, like the old Fisheries technical School and Celco High School in Baranghauon."[46]

"The house where Teodora Arana lived while estranged from her husband was inherited by Isidora Arana Villanueva (I) and eventually sold to Mrs. Concepcion Peña after the Second World War."[47] It became the Daniel B. Peña Memorial College, a Foundation, which is still functioning today. The foundation, together with the properties attached to it and unattached properties of Concepcion Rios Peña, which were retained after land reformed, are now under the control of Juanito Salvador Villanueva Rios (I), his wife, children and friend. He is the great-grand son of Vicente (I) and Mariano P.Villanueva (I); the grandson of Pedro Sr. (I) and Quiteria Villanueva (I); the third child and second son of Angela Villanueva Villanueva Rios Sr. (I) and Jesus Salvador Blance Rios (I).

"The house in Ermita, Malate was sold by Quiteria and she bought a two story house in Lourdes St., Pasay City."[48] The property in the town proper of Tabaco was sold to Mr. Ang Seng Yong and his descendants. The house of Pedro Sr. (I) and Quiteria (I) in Panal was ruined. Their youngest son, Jose V. Villanueva (I) built a house on the land and lived and manufactured wooden clogs and school desks until the business went bankrupt and part of the property was sold.

The daughters of Pedro Sr. (I) and Quiteria, Felicidad (I); Daria (I) and her son with Luis Madrid, Antonio (I); together with the children of Remedios (I) with Francisco de Lejos; and the daughter of Pedro Jr. (II), Elvira (I), lived in Pasay.

"Pasay" as it was fondly called became the "Home" away from home of most of the relatives of the Villanuevas while studying or vacationing in Manila or even while looking for work.

Virginia B. Malay wrote about Pasay City, particularly of Lourdes Street. Her article appeared on the Philipine Daily Inquirer titled "Saga of Lourdes Street". To quote some of the selected lines from the article: [49]

"Lourdes Street lies between Harrison St. and Roxas Boulevard...The houses were mostly chalet with nipa roof...The street was usually free of vehicles and we (children) could play on the street.

In the early 30s' a few Castillan families moved into Lourdes Street and built two story houses... In the middle of the 30s new wave of residents made their permanent abode in Lourdes St. They were mostly upper middle class, government officials and professionals. The Honorable Primitivo San Agustin Sr. who was the Secretary to the first President of the Philippine Commonwealth, his wife Doña Ruby and two sons...Priming and Tony who were with Doña Aurora Quezon when they were ambushed by the Huks in 1949.

The Maramba,... the Villa... During World War II some German Jew refugees from Nazi Germany lived in Lourdes.

During Liberation Pasay was burned down but the houses in Lourdes St. was miraculously spared. Aside from the original residents who still have their old houses standing there are the Villas and the Villanuevas of Bicol, the Coronados and the Reyeses..."

To read the complete article *"Saga of Lourdes Street"* by Virginia B. Malay, please refer to **Opinion**, Philippine Daily Inquirer, a cut out copy of which had been included here courtesy of Edna Lao Pasay City, MetroManila, Philippines.

Probably, one of the saddest part of the saga of the Villanueva was when one of the grandchildren of Mariano Sr. (I), Luz Villanueva de Lejos, one of the daughters of Remedios Villanueva de Lejos (I) " sold the ancestral cemetery plots including the headstones of the Villanuevas without the knowledge of other relatives. The bones, had been put together in an empty jars of mayonnaise." Eventually, the remains were sent to Tabaco to Muriel de Lejos Riosa for proper burial. [50]

Saga of Lourdes Street

HIGH BLOOD

Virginia B. Malay

WE'D also like to know the concerns of the sixtysomething and above, what makes their blood pressure rise or makes them sit back, content that all's well with their world and with themselves. —Ed.

REMINISCING brings fond recollections of childhood. I grew up in Pasay City, a town of Rizal in the mid-'20s. Pasay City then was idyllic and pristine—a far cry from the blighted city that it is now. After 40 years of the Cuneta administration, it has deteriorated a lot. It is disgustingly dirty and it has been called a "City of Sin" as well as a "squatters' paradise." I hope Sharon Cuneta, for all her charm and talent, does not make good her promise to run for mayor of Pasay City and instead give way to other aspiring and bona fide residents, who sincerely desire to serve our city and restore it to its old glory.

Lourdes Street lies between Harrison Street and Roxas Boulevard. When our family started living there, most of the houses were chalets with nipa roofs. There were just a few houses and, as children, we had a lot of space to play around. The street was usually free of vehicles and we could safely play *pico, patintero* and "kick the can" right on the street. Our environs were clean and we enjoyed the cool sea breeze of Manila Bay. What a joy it was to play and stroll on the beach, gather seashells and build castles on the sand. We would wade and jump over the waves in our street clothes, but got scolded by Mama for coming home all wet. Now the beach of our carefree years is the traffic-laden thoroughfare that Roxas Boulevard has become.

Different waves of residents have lived and left memories of their stay in Lourdes Street. During our early years, the neighborhood consisted of simple, indigenous and conservative people. We were comfortable with each other and our mothers observed such amenities as occasionally giving a neighbor a plate or bowl of cooked food from one's table for lunch or *merienda*.

In the early '30s, a few Castilian families moved into our street and built two-story houses. They could hardly speak Filipino and my parents put their knowledge of Spanish into good use. Our next-door neighbor, Doña Consuelo, lived alone with her dogs, which she pampered with Vienna bread and sausage. There was a tall guava tree laden with the sweetest guavas in her backyard. The Amechazuras were also our next neighbors. The daughters were our playmates and schoolmates at St. Paul's College, Manila. We imbibed some of their common Spanish expressions like, "*hasta la vista*," "*no me digas*," "*o y que?*" etc.

In middle '30s, a new wave of residents made their permanent abode in Lourdes Street. They were mostly upper middle class, government officials and professionals. The Honorable Primitivo San Agustin Sr. was secretary to the first President of the Philippine Commonwealth, Manuel L. Quezon. His wife, Doña Ruby was Mama's good friend. Her two sons, Priming and Tony were with Aurora A. Quezon and her family when they were ambushed by the Huks in 1949.

The Marambas were long-time residents of Lourdes. The Honorable Felix Maramba Sr. founded the very progressive Liberty Flour Mills. Larry Henares, a nephew, who lived with the Marambas for some time, often recalls his youthful experiences with my brother, Teddy and other friends, in his radio program and erstwhile column in the INQUIRER.

The Villas lived just across us and our families' friendship has been sustained through the years. But they are all gone and the only survivor is the former deputy ombudsman, Francisco Villa. His sister, Cynthia, never tired of retelling, before her untimely demise, how my brother, Teddy, would seek refuge at their place to escape my mother's fury over his escapades. Ms Villa and my mother were always distinguished by the mestiza dress they wore whenever they went to church and social affairs.

When the war broke out, the residents of Lourdes Street became closer yet, having plenty of time to socialize since most schools and offices were closed. Some German Jew refugees from Nazi Germany during World War II also lived in Lourdes Street during the Japanese Occupation. They seemed wealthy and educated people and we had friends among them too.

During the Liberation of Pasay, most of the houses were burned down, but the houses on Lourdes Street were miraculously spared. Since the holocaust took place on Feb. 11, 1945—the feast of Our Lady of Lourdes—the miracle was naturally attributed to her. Mama initiated the celebration of a thanksgiving Mass on the feast of Our Lady of Lourdes in the patio of our house, where we have a grotto of Lourdes. The tradition has been carried on up to the present, although now the Mass is celebrated on the street because the squatters who have invaded Lourdes, also join. The Mass is followed by a procession around the block. The parish priest, the barangay captain and some neighbors have dinner at home after the procession. Today, however, the squatters have made the tradition as their fiesta. Since they are now part of the community, they feel they belong.

Aside from us, the only original residents who still have their old houses standing there are the Villas, the Villanuevas of Bicol, the Coronados and the Reyeses. The well-appointed house of the San Agustins is now a nightspot with questionable activities.

The original residents who have left Lourdes Street felt sad to leave the place because they had spent a good many years of their lives there. Many of them moved to the subdivisions in Makati and Parañaque for the ambience that Lourdes Street had lost.

Our house is now hemmed in by a row of squatters on one side and a three-story condominium on the other side. Vehicles can hardly pass between parked tricycles, cars and jeepneys operated by the squatters. All kinds of stores—a barbershop and beauty parlor, as well as a makeshift funeral parlor occupy one side of the street. Children and infants play and roam around the place. Yet, in spite of all these irritants, my sisters have stayed on for convenience, because of its location. My oldest sister has actually expressed the wish to continue living in the Lourdes house until it's time for her to go.

Even in our twilight years now, we who have survived—seven siblings all—cling fondly to the house in Lourdes Street. It has seen us through significant events in our lives—from the day we were born to our growing-up years, schooling and graduation from elementary to college; World War II; the death of loved ones; happy times and heartaches. Be it ever so humble, the house on Lourdes Street will always be "Home Sweet Home."

Virginia B. Malay, 80, is a retired college professor.

Fig. 4. The article of Professor Malay

Notes and Sources

Introduction

Page xiii:

¹ Owen, Norman G., *The Bikol Blend and Their History*, 1999, Quezon City, Philippines: New Day Publishers, #11 Lands Street, VASRA/, P.O. Box 1167, 1100; p. 243.

² Rios, Angela Villanueva Villanueva Sr. (I); wife of Jesus Salvador Blance Rios Sr.; youngest daughter of Pedro Arana Villanueva Sr. (I) and Queteria Mabihis Villanueva (I); granddaughter of Vicente Villanueva (I) and (?) Mabihis; granddaughter of Mariano P. Villanueva (I) and Teodora Arana; excerpt from 1983 interview.

³ Buritt, Charles H. , First Lieutenant, Eleventh Cavalry, U. S. V., Officer in Charge The Mining Bureau, *The Coal Measure of the Philippines, A Rapid History of the Discovery of Coal in the Archipelago and Subsequent Developments, with the Full Text of the Record of the MaCleod Coal Concession in Cebu, or The Ulang-Lutac Coal and Railway Concession* by ; 1901, Washington: Government Printing Office, p. 175.

⁴ Morales, Orestes Murillo (I); husband of Dolores Dy Alparce; son of Enrique Villanueva Morales (I) and Trinidad Murillo, grandson of Candida Arana Villanueva (I) and Ramon Morales; great grandson of Mariano P. Villanueva Sr. (I) and Teodora Arana; as told by Fermin Ante Villanueva (I); husband of Anita (¿) and "Laleng" (¿); son of Delfin Arana Villanueva (I) and Pura Ante; grandson of Mariano P. Villanueva (I) and Teodora Arana.

⁵ Torres, Consuelo Bautista Villanueva Jr. (II); wife of Melqueides Torres Sr.; youngest daughter of Mariano Arana Villanueva Jr. (II) and Consuelo Bautista Sr.; granddaughter of Mariano P. Villanueva (I) and Teodora Arana; excerpt from interview done in California in the later part of 1980's.

⁶ Owen, Norman G., *The Bikol Blend and Their History,* 1999, Quezon City, Philippines: New Day Publishers, #11 Lands Street, VASRA/, P.O. Box 1167, 1100, p. 243.

Page xiv:

⁷ ibid.

⁸ ibid.

⁹ Owen, Norman G., *Prosperity Without Progress*, 1984, United States of America, The Regents of the University of California, University of California Press, Berkeley and Los Angeles, California, University of California Press, Ltd., London, England, p. 214.

Page xv:

[10] Foreign Office, *Miscellaneous Series, No. 197, Report on Subjects of General Interest and Commercial Interest. SPAIN. Report on Hemp Cultivation in the Philippine Islands*; 1891, London, Printed for Her Majesty's Stationary Office, Harrison and Sons, St Martin's Lane, Printers In Ordinary to Her Majesty.

Page xvi:

[11] Morales, Orestes Murillo (I); husband of Dolores Dy Alparce; son of Enrique Villanueva Morales (I) and Trinidad Murillo; grandson of Candida Arana Villanueva (I) and Ramon Morales; great grandson of Mariano P. Villanueva (I) and Teodora Arana; conversation at the birthday party of Andres Villanueva Rios (II) in Monrovia, California on April 24, 2011.

[12] Buenconsejo, Margarita de Lejos; wife of Anastacio Buenconsejo Sr.; daughter of Remedios Villanueva Villanueva (I) and Francisco de Lejos; granddaughter of Pedro Arana Villanueva Sr. (I) and Quiteria Mabihis Villanueva (I); great-granddaughter of Vicente Villanueva (I) (?) Mabihis; great granddaughter of Mariano P. Villanueva (I) and Teodora Arana ; 2014 telephone interview while she was in Pasay City, Metro Manila, Philippines.

[13] Rios, Angela Villanueva Villanueva Sr. (I); wife of Jesus Salvador Blance Rios Sr.; youngest daughter of Pedro Arana Villanueva Sr. (I) and Quiteria Mabihis Villanueva (I); granddaughter of Vicente Villanueva (I) and (?) Mabihis; granddaughter of Mariano P. Villanueva (I) and Teodora Arana; excerpt from 1983 interview.

[14] Riosa, Muriel de Lejos; wife of Santiago Villanueva Riosa Sr. (II).; daughter of Remedios Villanueva Villanueva (I) and Francisco de Lejos; ; granddaughter of Pedro Arana Villanueva Sr. (I) and Quiteria Mabihis Villanueva (I); granddaughter of Francisca Arana Villanueva (I); great-granddaughter of Vicente Villanueva (I) and (?) Mabihis; great granddaughter of Mariano P. Villanueva (I) and Teodora Arana; 2014 long distance telephone interview while she was in Tayhi, Tabaco, Albay Philippines.

[15] Common knowledge

[16] Rios, Angela Villanueva Villanueva Sr. (I); wife of Jesus Salvador Blance Rios Sr.; youngest daughter of Pedro Arana Villanueva Sr. (I) and Quiteria Mabihis Villanueva (I); granddaughter of Vicente Villanueva (I) and (?) Mabihis; granddaughter of Mariano P. Villanueva (I) and Teodora Arana; excerpt from 1983 interview.

[17] Buenconsejo, Margarita de Lejos; wife of Anastacio Buenconsejo Sr.; daughter of Remedios Villanueva Villanueva (I) and Francisco de Lejos; ; granddaughter of Pedro Arana Villanueva Sr. (I) and Quiteria Mabihis Villanueva (I); great-granddaughter of Vicente Villanueva (I) and (?) Mabihis; great granddaughter of Mariano P. Villanueva (I) and Teodora Arana. 2014 long distance telephone interview while she was in Pasay City, Metro Manila, Philippines.

[18] Buritt, Lt. Charles H., First Lieutenant, Eleventh Cavalry, U.S. V., Officer in Charge The Mining Bureau; *The Coal Measure of the Philippines, A Rapid History of the Discovery of Coal in the Archipelago and Subsequent Developments, with the Full Text of the Record of the MaCleod Coal Concession in Cebu, or The Ulang-Lutac Coal and Railway Concession* Washington, Government Printing Office, 1901, pp. 174 - 175.

[19] Rios, Angela Villanueva Villanueva Sr. (I); wife of Jesus Salvador Blance Rios Sr.; youngest daughter of Pedro Arana Villanueva Sr. (I) and Quiteria Mabihis Villanueva (I); granddaughter of Vicente Villanueva (I) and (?) Mabihis; granddaughter of Mariano P. Villanueva (I) and Teodora Arana; excerpt from 1983 interview.

[20] Daza, Nora Villanueva *with Family and Friends, Festive Dishes*, Edited by Michaela Fenix, 2011, Manila, Anvil Publishing, Inc., p. 38

Page xvii:

[21] Buritt, Lt. Charles H., First Lieutenant, Eleventh Cavalry, U.S. V., Officer in Charge The Mining Bureau; *The Coal Measure of the Philippines, A Rapid History of the Discovery of Coal in the Archipelago and Subsequent Developments, with the Full Text of the Record of the MaCleod Coal Concession in Cebu, or The Ulang-Lutac Coal and Railway Concession,* 1901, Washington, Government Printing Office, pp. 174 - 175.

[22] Sawyer, Frederick H., *Inhabitants of the Philippines*, 1900, London, Sampson Low, Marston and Company, pp. 154-155.

Page xviii:

[23] Halstead, Murat, *The Story of the Philippines and Our New Possessions Including The Ladrones, Hawaii, Cuba and Porto Rico*; 1898: Chicago Illinois, U.S.A., Our Possession Publishing Company; p. 343.

[24] 1953, Bureau of Public School, *History and Cultural Development of Barrio Batan*, Collected In Compliance with Executive Order No. 486, December 7, 1951 as embodied in General Memorandum No. 34, s. 1952.

[25] 2018 Google satelitte image of the islands of Rapu-Rapu and Batan.

[26] 1953, Bureau of Public School, *History and Cultural Development of Barrio Batan*, Collected In Compliance with Executive Order No. 486, December 7, 1951 as embodied in General Memorandum No. 34, s. 1952.

Page xix:

[27] ibid.

Page xx:

[28] Rios, Angela Villanueva Villanueva Sr. (I); wife of Jesus Salvador Blance Rios Sr.; youngest daughter of Pedro Arana Villanueva Sr. (I) and Quiteria Mabihis Villanueva (I); granddaughter of Vicente Villanueva (I) and (?) Mabihis; granddaughter of Mariano P. Villanueva (I) and Teodora Arana; excerpt from 1983 interview.

[29] ibid

Page xxi:

[30] Rios, Jaime Miguel Villanueva (I); husband of Amelia (Bebot) Fragante; 7th child and 4th son of Angela Villanueva Villanueva Rios Sr. (I) and Jesus Salvador Blance Rios Sr.; grandson of Pedro Arana Villanueva Sr. (I) and Quiteria Mabihis Villanueva (I); great grand son of Vicente Villanueva (I) and (?) Mabihis; great grandson of Mariano P. Villanueva (I) and Teodora Arana; excerpt from a 1991 conversation during a visit to the Philippines.

[31] Rios, Angela Villanueva Villanueva Sr. (I); wife of Jesus Salvador Blance Rios Sr.; youngest daughter of Pedro Arana Villanueva Sr. (I) and Quiteria Mabihis Villanueva (I); granddaughter of Vicente Villanueva (I) and (?) Mabihis; granddaughter of Mariano P. Villanueva (I) and Teodora Arana; excerpt from 1983 interview.

[32] Owen, Dr. Norman G., *Prosperity Without Progress,* 1984, United States of America, University of California Press, Berkely and Los Angeles California, University of California Press Ltd. London, England by The Regents of the University of California, p. 214.

[33] ibid.

[34] Philippine Supreme Court: *.G.R. No. L-7309 , October 10, 1913, MIGUEL BERSES and 318 others, plaintiff-appellants, vs.MARIANO P. VILLANUEVA, defendant-appellee.Singson, Ledesma and Lim, and Tirso de Irureta Goyena for appellants. Manly and McMahon for appellee.)*

[35] Morales, Orestes Murillo (I); husband of Dolores Dy Alparce; son of Enrique Villanueva Morales (I) and Trinidad Murillo; grandson of Candida Arana Villanueva (I) and Ramon Morales; great grandson of Mariano P. Villanueva (I) and Teodora Arana; conversation at the birthday party of Andres Villanueva Rios (II) in Monrovia, California on April 24, 2011.

Page xxii:

[36] Wood, Maria Leticia Patricia Villanueva Rios; wife of Charles Wood; oldest child and daughter of Angela Villanueva Villanueva Sr. (I) and Jesus Salvador B. Rios Sr.; granddaughter of Pedro Arana Villanueva Sr. (I) and Quiteria Mabihis Villanueva; great granddaughter of Vicente Villanueva (I) and (?) Mabihis; great granddaughter of Mariano P. Villaueva (I) and Teodora Arana.

[37] Rios, Angela Villanueva Villanueva Sr. (I); wife of Jesus Salvador Blance Rios Sr.; youngest daughter of Pedro Arana Villanueva Sr. (I) and Quiteria Mabihis Villanueva (I); granddaughter of Vicente Villanueva (I) and (?) Mabihis; granddaughter of Mariano P. Villanueva (I) and Teodora Arana; excerpt from 1983 interview.

[38] Alip, Dr. Eufronio Melo, *Poitical and Cultural History of the Philippines, Vol. II, since the British Occupation,* 1949, Manila, Philippines, Alip and Sons Inc., p. 260.

[39] Catalogo de la Exposicion General de las Islas Filipinas, Celebrada en Madrid, el 30 de Junio 1887; Group 18, pp. 289, 347, 371, 472, 496, 526, 542.

[40] Owen, Dr Norman G., *The Bikol Blend and Their History*, 1999, Quezon City, Philippines, New Day Publishers, #11 Lands Street, VASRA/, P.O. Box 1167, 1100, p. 245.

[41] Morales, Orestes Murillo; ; husband of Dolores Dy Alparce; oldest son of Enrique Villanueva Morales (I) and Trinidad Murillo; grandson of Candida Arana Villanueva (I) and Ramon Morales; great - grandsons of Mariano P. Villanueva (I) and Teodora Arana; April 24, 2011 conversation at the birthday party of Andres Villanueva Rios (II) in Monrovia, California.

[42] Public Information.

[43] Rios, Carlos Manuel Villanueva Sr. (I), husband of Emma Peralta; 5th child and 3rd son of Angela Villanueva Villanueva Sr. (I) and Jesus Salvador Blance Rios Sr.; grandson of Pedro Arana Villanueva Sr. (I) and Quiteria Mabihis Villanueva (I); great grandson of Vicente Villanueva (I) and (?) Mabihis; great grandson of Mariano P. Villanueva (I) and Teodora Arana; excerpt from a 2017 telephone conversation.

Page xxiii:

[44] Rios, Angela Villanueva Villanueva Sr. (I); wife of Jesus Salvador Blance Rios Sr.; youngest daughter of Pedro Arana Villanueva Sr. (I) and Quiteria Mabihis Villanueva (I); granddaughter of Vicente Villanueva (I) and (?) Mabihis; granddaughter of Mariano P. Villanueva (I) and Teodora Arana; excerpt from 1983 interview.

Page xxiv:

[45] Common knowledge among older generation of the town of Tabaco

[46] Riosa, Muriel Villanueva de Lejos (I), wife of Santiago Estevez Riosa Sr. (II); daughter of Remedios Villanueva Villanueva and Francisco de Lejos; granddaughter of Pedro Arana Villanueva Sr. (I) and Quiteria Mabihis Villanueva (I); great-granddaughter of Vicente Villanueva (I) and (?) Mabihis; great granddaughter of Mariano P. Villanueva (I) and Teodora Arana.

[47] Rios, Angela Villanueva Villanueva Sr. (I); wife of Jesus Salvador Blance Rios Sr.; youngest daughter of Pedro Arana Villanueva Sr. (I) and Quiteria Mabihis Villanueva (I); granddaughter of Vicente Villanueva (I) and (?) Mabihis; granddaughter of Mariano P. Villanueva (I) and Teodora Arana; excerpt from 1983 interview.

[48] ibid.

Page xxv:

[49] Malay, Dr. Virginia, *Saga of Lourdes Street*, n.d., Philippine Daily Inquirer, Opinion, Article contributed by Mrs.Edna Lao of Pasay, Metromanila, Philippines

[50] Lao, Edna de Lejos Buenconsejo (I); widow of Ricardo Lao; daughter of Margarita Villanueva de Lejos (I) and Anastacio Buenconsejo Sr.; granddaughter of Remedios Villanueva Villanueva and Francisco de Lejos; great granddaughter of Pedro Arana Villanueva Sr. (I) and Quiteria Mabihis Villanueva (I); great-great granddaughter of Vicente Villanueva (I) and (?) Mabihis; great great granddaughter of Mariano P. Villanueva (I) and Teodora Arana; excerpt from 2016 telephone conversation while she is in Pasay City, MetroManila, Philippines.

Chapter I

Vicente Villanueva (I)

DOD 1891

Not much had been known about Vicente (I) except that he was the brother and business partner of Mariano Villanueva Sr. (I). He lived in Legaspi, Albay but also maintained a house in Malate, Manila.

According to his granddaughter, Angela Villanueva Rios Sr.(I), he had three "*hijas y hijo naturales*"[1] with a lady surnamed Mabihis.[2] When the lady died and the children were grown-up, he married a very beautiful Filipino-Spanish lady named (Thomas?) Tomas also from Legaspi and had one son with her named, Balbino.

Some people of Tabaco raised the question that the mother of the first three children, Mabihis, was probably the maid employed in the household of Vicente (I). No recollection and record of the lady is available except that she had a brother named Rafael Mabihis living in Legaspi.[3]

The children with Mabihis were Quiteria, (pictured below) Antonio and Maria (I). Quiteria married her first cousin Pedro Arana Villanueva (I), the oldest son of Mariano P. Villanueva (I), brother of Vicente P. Villanueva (I).[4]

In 1896, Antonio, who was studying in Hong Kong came back to help and support the revolution. He died at the age of 20 in the battle of Tirad Pass against the Americans with General Gregorio del Pilar who was not that much older than him. He was said to be the first to deliver a revolutionary speech in English. The body was never recovered.[5]

Maria (I) was studying at the convent, La Concordia, in Manila when the revolution started. The family in Legaspi, having no communications and had no way of finding out if

Fig. 5 Quiteria M. Villanueva

the students had been evacuated, could not send the much needed allowance for her maintenance. Neglected, she contracted tuberculosis. Immediately after the war ended, Quiteria, looked and found her sister in the convent too ill to move. She was immediately taken back to Tabaco to be nursed back to health but she never recovered from the affliction and died. She was buried in Tabaco.[6]

Vicente (I) and Thomas had a son named Balbino who was said to be very handsome. Balbino had an affair with an Englishwoman and had a son named Victor who was as handsome as his father.

Victor lived in England and became a professor in one of the Universities in London, England. Ernestina Salcedo met Victor during her travels in Europe.[7]

On June 30 of 1887, Vicente gave the following items to be exhibited at the Philippine General Exposition in Madrid:

(1887, Catalogo de Exposicion de las Islas Filipinas en Madrid de 30 de Junio, 1887, pp. 289, 496, 542).

Section 2, Group 18, p. 289.[8]

104. A local wooden saddle used by the indegenous people of both sexes and another saddle for ladies.

Group 49, Section 7, p. 496.[9]

55. Two rolls of hawser. (thick cable or rope used in mooring or towing ships)

Group 53, p. 542.[10]

104. Five wallets made of nito

On May 15, 1889, Vicente became the godfather of the 27-year-old Chinese, Santiago Villanueva Te Sunco of Tiui, who was baptized as a Catholic by Fr. Prudencio Santos, curate of the town of Tiui. The baptism was certified on May 19 of the same year.

Santiago Villanueva Te Sunco was a native of Chingcang, China and a resident of Tiui. Vicente was represented by his brother, Mariano P. Villanueva (I).[11]

When Vicente (I) died in 1891 (1998, Owen, p.245) "his estate was valued at P200,000."[12] His properties were divided equally to his wife, only surviving oldest daughter, Quiteria, and to his son, Balbino. Balbino took his inheritance, moved and lived in Spain with his mother. No relatives had heard anything about them afterwards.

Mariano (I) became the administrator of Quiteria's inheritance, which included her father's share of the Messrs. Villanueva & Co. holdings in the coal mine of Batan Island.[13]

Quiteria did not get all of her inheritance because Mariano P. (I) disposed most of them in his favor. So that she could not inherit her share of "Minas de Batan", Mariano sold the mines and kept the proceeds. At the time it was not customary to sue relatives over money and cause embarrassment for the family. Besides Quiteria's husband and her were already very rich in their own right.[14]

Genealogical Line of Vicente Villanueva

1st Gen:— Vicente Villanueva (I) - +n.m. - Mabihis

                           I

2nd Gen: a. Quiteria - +m. Pedro Villanueva Sr. (I)

                b. Maria (I)   - died, single, end of line

                c. Antonio (I)   - died, single, end of line

1st Gen:- Vicente Villanueva (I) +m. Thomas

    2nd Gen: a. Balbino (I) - +n.m. Unnamed Englishwoman

                        I

    3rd Gen: a. Victor Villanueva (I)

Notes and Sources

Chapter I

Page 1:

¹ Rios, Angela Villanueva Villanueva Sr. (I); wife of Jesus Salvador Blance Rios Sr.; youngest daughter of Pedro Arana Villanueva Sr. (I) and Quiteria M. Villanueva (I); granddaughter of Vicente Villanueva (I) and (?) Mabihis; granddaughter of Mariano P. Villanueva (I) and Teodora Arana. Excerpt from a 1983 interview.

² Riosa, Muriel Villanueva De Lejos (I); wife of Santiago Villanueva Riosa Sr. (II); daughter of Remedios Villanueva Villanueva (I) and Francisco de Lejos; granddaughter of Pedro Arana Villanueva Sr. (I) and Quiteria Mabihis Villanueva (I); great-granddaughter of Vicente Villanueva (I) and (?) Mabihis; great granddaughter of Mariano P. Villanueva (I) and Teodora Arana: as transmitted by Villar, Corina Belle Riosa, daughter of Evelyn de Lejos Riosa and Edwin Villar; granddaughter of Santiago Villanueva Riosa Sr. (II) and Muriel Villanueva de Lejos (I); great granddaughter of Magin Villanueva Riosa Sr. (I) and Purificacion Estevez; great granddaughter of Remedios Villanueva Villanueva (I) and Francisco de Lejos; great - great-granddaughter of Pedro Arana Villanueva Sr. (I) and Quiteria Mabihis Villanueva (I); great-great granddaughter of Francisca Arana Villanueva and Santiago Riosa (I); great-great-great granddaughter of Vicente Villanueva (I) and (?) Mabihis; great-great-great granddaughter of Mariano P. Villanueva (I) and Teodora Arana.

³ ibid…

⁴ ⁻ Rios, Angela Villanueva Villanueva Sr. (I); wife of Jesus Salvador Blance Rios Sr.; youngest daughter of Pedro Arana Villanueva Sr. (I) and Quiteria Mabihis Villanueva (I); granddaughter of Vicente Villanueva (I) and (?) Mabihis; granddaughter of Mariano P. Villanueva (I) and Teodora Arana. Excerpt from a 1983 interview.

⁵ ibid

Page 2:

⁶ ibid

⁷ Rios, Angela Villanueva Villanueva Sr. (I); wife of Jesus Salvador Blance Rios; youngest daughter of Pedro Arana Villanueva Sr. (I) and Quiteria Mabihis Villanueva (I); granddaughter of Vicente Villanueva (I) and (?) Mabihis; granddaughter of Mariano P. Villanueva (I) and Teodora Arana: Excerpt from a 1983 interview; as told by Salcedo,

Ernestina Quijano (I); daughter of Melania Quijano and (?) Salcedo; granddaughter of Mariano P. Villanueva (I) and (n.m.) "Lanyang" Quijano.

[8] 1887, June 30, *Catálogo de la Exposicion General de las Islas Filipinas, Celebrada en Madrid, Inaugarada Por M. La Reina Regente. El 30 de Junio de 1887*; Madrid: Est. Tipografico de Ricardo Fé, Calle Cedaceros, núm 11, 1887, p, *Catalogo de Exposicion de las Islas Filipinas en Madrid*, pp. 289, 496, 542.

[9] ibid., p. 496,

[10] ibid., p. 542

[11] Philippine National Archive N.O. 199.387/#208; N.O.210.804/ #208; SDS#2595 (Bautismos: Albay).

[12] Owen, Dr. Norman G., *The Bikol Blend and Their History*, 1999, Quezon City, Philippines, New Day Publishers, #11 Lands Street, VASRA/, P.O. Box 1167, 1100, p. 243.

[13] Rios, Angela Villanueva Villanueva Sr. (I); wife of Jesus Salvador Blance Rios Sr.; youngest daughter of Pedro Arana Villanueva Sr. (I) and Quiteria Mabihis Villanueva (I); granddaughter of Vicente Villanueva (I) and (?) Mabihis; granddaughter of Mariano P. Villanueva (I) and Teodora Arana . Excerpt from a 1983 interview.

Page 3:

[14] ibid.,

Chapter II

Mariano Porferio Villanueva (I)

1843 – April 22, 1918

Mariano Sr. (I), based on the stories of his descendants, lived a more colorful life than his brother, Vicente (I). He married the beautiful Teodora Arana, a lady from Albay, Legaspi City[1] in 1867[2]. They lived in the house facing Bonifacio Street, which was later sold to Smith Bell & Co., which in turn, was sold to Angela Manalang Gloria, the poet Laureate of Tabaco. The descendant of Angela Manalang Gloria converted it to a museum.

Mariano (I) and Teodora had other houses in Tabaco, which included the one behind the Tabaco Municipal building, which was later owned by the Lao Kiat family. The building of the Peña Memorial College was the house where Teodora sought refuge when she was estranged from her philandering husband.

Concepcion Rios Peña, the sister in-law of Angela Villanueva Rios Sr. (I), bought the house from Isidora who inherited it from her father, Mariano (I). Isidora (I) was the only ligitimate child of Mariano (I) and Teodora who had sided with her father and his mistress "*Lanyang Quijano*",[3] when Teodora and Mariano (I) separated.

Fig. 6. Mariano P. Villanueva's ancestral house taken in 1992.

Mariano P. (I) had ten children with Teodora. Court records say that beside from his mistress *"Lanyang"* Quijano, Mariano P. (I) had several relationships with other women and had illegitimate children with them. Six of the illegitimate children were named, five of whom were from his mistress *"Lanyang"* Quijano.[4] The rest of the illegitimate children were not known. *"Lanyang "*Quijano used to be Mariano P.'s girlfriend before he married Teodora Arana. He had a continuing relationship with her from 1868 until 1900;

"In 1889 and 1890 he had an adulterous relationship with a woman and had a daughter named Maria (III) who bore his name. The mother of Maria (III) died during the American occupation. In 1891, Mariano (I) had another adulterous relationship with another woman. No children were mentioned. In 1892, until Teodora filed for a divorce in 1910, he had a relationship with a woman who bore him children. In 1901 and 1902, he had another relationship with a woman and again in the years 1903 and 1904 with a different woman. No children were mentioned."[5]

At the Tabaco Catholic Cemetery, there is a tombstone, which has the name of Balbino B. Villanueva. He was born on March 31, 1896 and died on June 6, 1946. Further research using Ancestry.com revealed that he was the son of Mariano P. Villanueva and Quiteria Buenconsejo,[6] although his name was not mentioned at the Supreme Court Record during the Divorce case of Teodora Arana vs. Mariano P. Villanueva (I) of 1910.

On June 30 1887, Mariano P. (I) contributed to the exhibit at the Exposicion General de las Islas Filipinas in Madrid, (1887, Catálogo de la Exposicion General de las Islas Filipinas de 1887 celebrada en Madrid, p. 371), the following items under #208 presented by the Royal Economic Society: *nito* and *Piña*.[7]

On page 472 under Group 45, #595 of the same Catalogue: Mariano P. (I) exhibited, **a.** café una nuestra con cascara abaca; se utilizan sus fibras en la fabricacion de curdas; cables y tejidos finisimos. (Sample of coffee with abaca shell; the fibers of which is used in the production of cords, cables and fine thread. **b.** Cacao una muestra (sample of cacao) **c.** algodon en rama (cotton on a branch).[8]

On page 526 under Group 50: **a.** tejido de Piña (Pineapple fiber); **b.** tejido de abaca imitando seda (abaca fiber imitating silk).[9]

On page 542 of the Catálogo, under Group 53, #103 **a.** un salacot de *nito*, (a hat made of *nito* **b.** tres pitacas de *nito* (three wallet made of *nito*).[10]

Known for his fiery temper, he carried a whip (latigo), which he used freely for any infraction.[11] He went about town in his carriage drawn by six horses and driven by a servant. Whenever he sees a woman that he liked, he would send his servant to investigate where she lived and then the next day he would visit the woman with a land title in his hand to bribe her with it so he can have relationship with her.[12] According to some old people, he made womanizing "fashionable" for rich people in the town of Tabaco.[13]

He was a good, calculating businessman. He and his brother Vicente (I) started a very successful business buying and selling *sinamay* and other hemp products in Bicol. They owned holdings of Coal mine in Batan Island and according to their granddaughter, Angela Villanueva Rios Sr. (I), they also were part owner of a gold mine.[14] So far, no records had been found to support this claim that the Villanueva brothers were part owners of a gold mine. The Company that he and his brother owned had a cargo ship,[15] which also served as passengers' transport for members of the family vacationing from Manila.[16]

He was measly as well as generous. He donated the land for the municipal building of Tabaco.[17] He and his family also donated a big bell for the bell tower of the Catholic stone church of the town.[18] The bell, although crack, still exists in the bell tower of the original stone Catholic Church of Tabaco.

Mariano P. (I) served three terms as *Governadorcillo* of Tabaco. His first term was in 1879-1880. He served again in 1883-1884 and later in 1889.[19] Dr. Owen commented (1999, Bikol Blend: Bikolanos and their History, p. 238),[20]

"The assertion that the real Filipino leaders shunned the posts of cabeza and even gobernadorcillo is made by Govantes y Azcáraga, 564, Casademunt, 51-54, and Millan, 117-129, among many others. It has become a commonplace of Philippine history without, to my knowledge, ever having been tested. Such avoidance may well have taken place in the Tagalog areas close to Manila, where the process of commercialization, modernization and alienation seem to have been further advanced, but there is no evidence it was happening in Kabikolan. Although there is no disproving the theoretical possibility of rich families who kept their influence well hidden, almost all the identifiable Bikol elite held municipal posts at one time or another. Some seemingly tried to become gobernadorcillo quickly, and thus principales for life (as capitanes pasados), but Mariano P. Villanueva of Tabaco-who had already been gobernadorcillo-was still serving as a cabeza de barangay in 1891 when he was sole manager and half owner of Villanueva & Co. a firm worth over P400,000; PNA, Protocoles, Albay, 1026."

The people of San Miguel Island who felt that he illegally took their lands cursed Mariano P. (I) and his descendants up to the 3rd generation.[21] Although, in his defense, his grandchildren, said that the land in San Miguel, about 1300 hectares[22], was given to him by the Spanish authority for his public service as part of the *encomienda* system.[23] but according to court records, on November 1, 1890, he received a grant of 1300 hectares of uncultivated royal land in San Miguel Island, through adjustment, from the Spanish government with the understanding that the said land *"was unappropriated and not in the legal possession of anyone."* The title was officially registered on June 13, 1891 under the name of Mariano P. Villanueva (I). [24] It should be noted that King Philipi V abolished the encomienda system in 1720-1721, although its use continued to the eighteenth century.[25]

The "*curse of the Villanueva*" came about when Mariano (I) filed a complaint in court for the recovery of possession of a tract of land in the Island of San Miguel in March 1902. Two residents of San Miguel Island, Miguel Berses and Alejandro Brusola and nine other defendants were named in the complaint. Their cases No. 29 and No. 33 respectively were consolidated by order of the Judge in April 18,1903 which was then prosecuted as a single case. The initial total of hectares involved then was 14.[26]

However, on February 11, 1905, the defendants filed a motion and requested the court that besides representing themselves, they represent other persons interested in the case under the denomination "*inhabitant of the Island of San Miguel*" pursuant to section 118 of the Civil Code Procedure. More than three thousand (3,000) persons were now involved increasing the hectares in question to 1,300 which was practically the whole island.[27]

On December 3,1906 the court decided in favor of Mariano P. Villanueva (I). The Counsel for the defendants appealed the court decision. They filed a written complaint on November 20,1908 thus turning Mariano P. Villanueva (I) as defendant.

But on March 10, 1911 before the Philippine Supreme Court could decide on the case of Miguel Berses and 318 others, plaintiff-appellant vs. Mariano P. Villanueva (I), defendant-appellee, it rendered another decision involving Mariano P. Villanueva brought on by Manuel Cea. On the case of Manuel Cea, Plaintiff-appellant, vs. Mariano P. Vllanueva, Guillermo Gonzales, and the Provincial Sheriff, Leon Reyes, defendant-appelles. The entirety of the court case is as follows: [28]

Republic of the Philippines
Supreme court
Manila
G.R. No. 5446 March 10, 1911

MANUEL CEA, PLINTIFF-APPELLANT, VS. **MARIANO P. VILLANUEVA, GUILLERMO GONZALES AND the provincial sheriff, LEON RYES,** DEFENDANT-APPELLEES.

FUENTEBELLA AND CEA FOR APPELANT.
HAUSSERMANN, ORTIGAS, COHN AND FISHER FOR THE APPELLEES.

MORELAND, J.:

This is an appeal by the plaintiff from a judgment of the Court of First Instance of the Province of Ambos Camarines, Hon. Grant Trent presiding, absolving the defendants from the obligation charged in the complaint, with costs.—

This action has proceeded upon two theories: (1) Upon the theory that the defendants, having entered into the possession of a house and a lot, the property of the plaintiff, by gross negligence and carelessness, caused it to be burned to the damage of the plaintiff; and (2) upon the theory that the defendants entered into possession of a house and lot belonging to the plaintiff, knowing that they were not entitled to the possession thereof, and acting, therefore, in bad faith, they were responsible to the plaintiff for the destruction of the house by fire.

Upon the whole case we are clearly satisfied that neither of these theories has been sustained by the evidence and that the case was correctly decided by the learned trial court.—

It appears that in the year 1906 the defendant Villanueva began an action against the plaintiff to foreclose a mortgage, which he held upon various parcels of real estate belonging to the plaintiff, and prosecuted the same to final judgment. After waiting the proper time for the plaintiff to pay the indebtedness upon which the mortgage was based, and he not having made such payment, said parcels of land, under the terms of said judgment, were offered for public sale and were sold to said Villanueva at public auction on e 3rd day of September, 1906, he being the highest bidder at said sale. Thereafter and on the 12th day of September, of the same year, the said defendant, through the activities of the sheriff, entered into possession of the property, including one of the pieces of land called parcel No. 2. Upon delivering possession of said parcel No. 2 to the defendant Villanueva, the sheriff found that there was a house built upon said lot, which house was not specifically mentioned in the description of parcel No. 2, although the land upon which it stood was clearly within the description of said parcel as presented by the documents. Fearing that by reason of the failure of such description specifically to mention the house in question his power did not extend to the delivery of the possession of said house, the sheriff informed the defendants that, in the event that the court should determine that said house was not property embraced within the mortgage and legally conveyed under the mortgage sale, they, the defendants, must not only deliver possession but also pay to the plaintiff a proper sum for its occupancy. The employee of the plaintiff who had been in charge of the house up to the time of the delivery of its possession was then notified by the sheriff that he must quit the premises and that the defendant was to occupy them in instead. The employee, however, loath to leave uncared for certain articles that were there on the premises, asked permission of the sheriff to be permitted to remain there for the purpose of caring therefore. The sheriff informed him that he had no power to give such permission and referred him to the defendants. The latter immediately gave permission to the employee to remain upon the premises and look after the property referred to in his petition. The defendant placed an employee of his own in the possession of the property to care for and protect it from injury or destruction. On the 12th day of November of the same year the court before which the judgment of foreclosure and sale had been obtained, and which ordered the sale of said property under the said judgment for reasons which are immaterial here, annulled the sale and ordered a resale of the same. During the month of December the property described in the mortgage, including parcel No. 2 in question was again sold at public sale and again purchased by the defendant Villanueva. Prior to this time, however, and on the night of of the 3rd of October 1906, the house located on parcel No. 2 was destroyed by fire. The evidence does not disclose in what manner the fire originated or through whose fault or negligence, if of anyone, it occurred. Upon that question the record is wholly silent.

The first contention presented by the appellant to this court is that the learned trial court erred in holding that the house in question was included in the sale made by the sheriff under the judgment of foreclosure and sale.

We have carefully examined the record in connection with this allegation of error and are thoroughly satisfied that the evidence fully supports the conclusion of the learned trial court in this respect. It appears that the description of the land upon which the house was located is included within the description of parcel No. 2 in the mortgage referred to. The appellant in his complaint and in his argument presents a description of the house and lot referred to somewhat different in words from the description of parcel No. 2. This, however, causes no confusion, inasmuch as it is quite clear that the description of parcel No. 2 fully includes the house and lot described by the appellant.

The second contention of the appellant is that the learned trial court erred in finding that the possession of defendants of parcel No. 2, which includes the house and lot in question, was in good faith.

As to the contention, the record does not leave us in doubt. It having been found that the description contained in the mortgage includes the house and lot in question, the resolution of the present question is easy. In the case of *Bischoff vs. Pomar* (12 Phil.Rep., 690), this court held, Mr. Justice Torres writing the opinion, that –

> *It is a rule established by the Civil Code and also by the Mortgage Law, with which the decision of the courts of the United States are in accord, that in a mortgage of Real Estate, the improvements on the same are included; therefore, all objects permanently attached to a mortgage building or land, although they may have been placed there after the mortgage was constituted, are also included.*

The Civil Code, Article 1877, provides that –

> *A mortgage includes the natural accessions, improvements, growing fruits and rents not collected when the obligation is due. . . .(Manresa, vol. 12, pp.449,500).*

From this it is evident that the house in question passed under the mortgage sale. When, therefore, the defendant entered into possession thereof after he had purchased it at the foreclosure sale, he presumably entered into possession honestly and in good faith. That he did so is nowhere put in question by the evidence in this case. No direct evidence is given anywhere attacking his motives or his intentions. When the defendant took possession he did so as owner of the property and, even if he would still have been a holder in good faith, being a mortgage in possession under direction of the court.

> *Good faith is always presumed, and any person alleging bad faith on the part of the possessor is obliged to prove it. Possession acquired in good faith does not lose this character, except in the case and from the moment some acts exists proving that the possessor is aware that he possesses the thing illegally. It is presumed that the possession is still enjoyed in the manner in which it was acquires until the contrary is proved. (Arts. 434,435,436, Civil Code).)*

> *Where a purchaser at a defective foreclosure sale, or his assigns, goes into possession of the mortgaged premises, with assent of the mortgagor, under the right supposed to have been acquired under the foreclosure sale, he will be deemed a mortgagee in possession. (Russell vs. Akely Lum. Co., 45 Minn., 376; Rogers vs. Benton, 39 Minn., 39).-*

> *A purchase at a mortgage foreclosure sale, which is invalid as against the owner of the equity of redemption, becomes assignee of the mortgage, and if he lawfully enters into possession of the premises, he becomes a mortgagee in possession, and ejectment will not lie against him by the owner of the equity of redemption. (Townshend vs. Thomson 139 N. Y., 152)-*

> *An alienee of a mortgage, who claimed title under a foreclosure sale, acquires all the rights of a mortgagee, even though the foreclosure sale is void for irregularity, so as not to bar the equity of redemption. Being in the position of a mortgagee in possession after breach of condition with the debt unpaid, he has a good defense to an ejectment brought on the bare legal title. (Bryan vs. Brasius, 162 U.S. , 415)*

The defendant having entered into possession of the property lawfully, he was obligated to exercise only reasonable diligence and care in the management of the property. (Art. 1903, Civil Code; Wann vs. Coe, 31 Fed., 369; Murdock vs. Clark, 90 Cal., 427.)

Article 457 of the Civil Code reads as follows:

> *A possessor in good faith is not liable for the deterioration or loss of the thing possessed, with the exception of the cases in which it is proved that he has acted with fraudulent intent. A possessor in bad faith is liable for the deterioration or loss in any case, even in those caused by force majeure, when he has maliciously delayed the delivery of the thing to its legitimate possessor.*

It appearing from the nature of the relation of the defendant to the property that he was not a holder in bad faith, nor a usurper, he is responsible only for those losses, which are shown to have been caused by his negligence. No Negligence having been shown in this case the complaint was properly dismissed upon the merits.__

The Judgment is affirmed, without special findings as to costs. __

Arellano, C. J., Torres, Mapa and Carson, JJ., concur.

On October 10, 1913, the Philippine Supreme Court made the final decision on the case of Miguel Berses and 318 others, plaintiff-appelants vs. Mariano P. Villanueva, defendant-appelle.[29]

Republic of the Philippines
SUPREME COURT
Manila

EN BANC

G.R. No. L-7309   October 10, 1913

MIGUEL BERSES and 318 others, *plaintiff-appellants,*
vs.
MARIANO P. VILLANUEVA, *defendant-appellee.*

Singson, Ledesma and Lim, and Tirso de Irureta Goyena for appellants.
Manly and McMahon for appellee.

TORRES, J.:

Appeal raised, through bill of exceptions, by counsel for the plaintiffs from the judgment of January 28, 1910, whereby the former judge of the Eighth District, the Honorable Grant T. Trent, held that the plaintiffs were not entitled, either jointly or severally, to an award for improvements or for losses and damages, and dismissed their complaint with the costs against them proportionately, and absolved them from the counterclaim filed by the defendant.

On November 20, 1908, counsel for the plaintiffs filed a written complaint with the Court of First Instance of Albay, against Mariano P. Villanueva, wherein it was alleged that each of the plaintiffs had been and still was in possession of a tract of 1, 300 hectares of land situated in the Island of San Miguel, Tabaco, Albay, bounded on the north by the sea and the lands of Pedro Comel, Candido Banao, Alejandro Broce, Teodora Bondal, Mateo N. and Mariano Bonaobra; on the east and south, by the sea; and on the west, by the lands of Jose Bombales, Gregorio Breza, Jose Buenconsejo, Juan Bueno, Anacleto Bedolio,

Gregorio Rebollido, Alejandro Bonreales and Luis Buensalida; that each and all of the plaintiffs, in the belief that they were the owners of the said land, had thereon sown and planted grain and plants of different kinds, erected houses and other buildings and made other improvements, and planted coconuts, cacao, bananas, bamboo, nipa palm, coffee, lemon trees, sugar cane, abaca, anahao, gallang and caragomoy; that the names of each one of the plaintiffs and the total value of the plantings, crops, building and other improvements, were as follows: Miguel Berses, for the value of P22,382; Rufino Bogñalos, P6,325; Hipolito Bogñalos, P3, 665; Valentin Buela, P1,866.50; Arcadio Biraguit, P14,154; Dalmacio Buara, P2,411; Ciriaco Bongalon, P1,314.50; Fabian Para, P3,258; Doroteo Brosola, P1,354; Francisco Buara, P4,335; Hermogenes Batis, P1,243. 50; Ildefonso Buara, P3,827; Fermin Baina, P859; Pantaleon Buban, P1,556; Maximo Buara, P2,787.50; Lucio Bara, P685; Romualdo Buebos, P1,111; Paulino Buara, P1,360; Fermin Broso, P1,300; Alberto Santos, P1,122; Eufrasio Balinbing, P897.50; Norberto Broce, P154; Segundo Biraquit, P1,805.50; Bernardo Biraquit, P2,312; Ruperto Broso, P1,854; Pablo Bolima, P2,178; Fernando Buenconsejo, P864; Amaro Bonagua, P1,729; Sinforoso Madrid, P845; Leon Buison, P3,146.50; Vicente Bolda, P1,726.50; Lorenzo Sarmiento, P662.50; Evaristo Cal, P576; Maximino Bola, P1,285; Agaton Bore, P1,264; Basilio Lanon, P135; Cornelo Buara, P4,654.50; Francsco Brutas, P1,730; Antero Borbe, P3,747; Doroteo Bueno, P333; Juan Brutas, P642; Jose Buara, P1,327; Cenon Lanon, P2,623; Jose Biñocot, P275; Angelo Bucaya, P3,363; Epifanio Cortesano, P3,117; Nicolas Bonagua, P1,043; Florencio Bien, P290; Francisco Bolima, P938; Hipolito Vergara, P705; Jose Borbe, P258.50; Nemesio Cal, P440; Buenaventura Borcer, P459; Martina Bogay, P613; Graciano Bien, P230; Geronimo Camo, P965; Juan Bonagua, P1,036; Alejandro Bien, P3,094.50; Benito Bogñalbal, P513; Tomas Berlon, P2,559; Pedro Berlon, P1,284.50; Paulino Buara, P1,113; Sotera bien, P588; Eustaquio Cortesano, P1,359.50; Hermogenes Contrata, P590; Vcente Bueno, P3,330; Juan Buñales, P1,374; Micaela Buñaga, P1,750; Jacinto Dato, P859; Candido Bondad, P1,246. 50; Simeon Buising, P1,644.50; Arcado Bonaobra, P1,046; Narciso and Tomas Borboran, P2,371; Miguela Vista, P1,255; Silvino Vara, P800; Teodorico Brutas, P308; Raymundo Bongay, P633; Zuelo Bombeta, P178; Juan Bonagua, P6,962; Pedro Biron, P1,095; Teodoro Burac, P513; Maximo Bongalon, P2,660; Petrona Bongon, P1,472.50; Petrona Bongon, P315; Jacinto Brutas, P3,507; Felix Brutas, P1,771; Mariano Bodes, P876.50; Roman Cortesano, P2,093; Januario Busar, P1,169; Damaso Bonete, P4,433; Manuel Borbe, P788; Toribio Bonaobra, P2,040.50; Simeona Bien, P788; Petronilo Bradecina, P1,737; Roman Bolda, P689; Fausto Bredes, P1,919; Jacinto Basmayor, P4,630; Gregorio Prutas, P770; Eugenio Buela, P1,917.50; Sebastian Bordonada, P3,077; Hermenegildo Berlon, P188; Urbano Berlon, P5,568; Severino Borbe, P717; Faustino Duran, P593; Canuto Buñales, P4,088; Francisco Bitago, P1,509; Anastacio Bogñales, P1,474; Zacarias Bien, P512; Juan Rolisan, P1,990; Clemente Relisan, P519; Teresa Bocaya, P471.50; Brigido Borbe, P708; Bonifacio Bondad, P1,516; Isaac Bontigas, P364;

Prudencio Bolima, P1,311; Josefa Bredes, P767.50; Escolastico Briquillo, P576; Narciso Balingbing, P962; Florentino Barra, P748; Juan Barra, P358; Basilio Borce, P2,889; Francisco Borac, P330; Rufino Bongay, P3,355; Juan Bueno, P1,504; Florentino Barra, P873; Juan Barra, P297; Pablo Brutas, P790; Mariano Agunday, P711; Mariano Brisuela, P454; Silvino Barra, P957; Lorenzo Bien, P506; Vicente Barra, P437; Julio Bugñalos, P781; Eulogio Brondo, P2,742; Albino Buevos, P661; Gabriel Bueno, P1,758; Apolinario Bigino, P1,157; Leon Bueno, P555; Juan Borbe, P1,922; Marcos Bradecina, P7,371; Alberto Bredes, P5,825; Teofilo Burcer, P337; Hermenegildo Marquez, P477; Santiago Bola, P765.50; Mariano Bonagua, P2,022; Nicolas Buensalida, P1,015; Jacobo Buison, P1,641; Juan Bonagua, P1,299; Zacarias Berces, P2,651.50; Pantaleon Bueno, P1,939; Candido Bondad, P3,734; Eulalio Bolima, P191.50; Arcadio Bueno, P628; Juan Flores, P1,325; Juan Brosola, P992; Juan Busmayor, P3,069; Marcelino Brosola, P662; Mariano Agunday, P2,774.50; Francisco Bueno, P1,786; Perfecto Billa, P1,013; Victor Brosola, P6,059; Sotero Briquillo, P850; Valentin Baina, P1,112; Agaton Boragay, P970; Juan Buna, P589; Atanacio Buising, P840; Leoncio Bien, P496; Serapio Bueco, P770; Raymundo Bongay, P91; Valerio Bonganay, P563.50; Teodoro Jacob, P2,371; Susana Urnan, P716; Tomas Billa, P193; Pedro Bonaobra, P760; Antonio Barquin, P636; Jose Bien, P465; Pedro Corral, P350; Baldomero Bayobo, P722; Bernardo Gandul, P158; Basilia Boragay, P353; Pedro Boticario, P1,616; Maria Cañon, P744; Maximo Blanquesa, P1,566; Manuel Broso, P244; Alberto Bongay, P274; Esteban Buela, P1,089.50; Fermin Bigcas, P524; Marcos Brutas, P1,281; Mariano Bolo, P366,50; Pablo Bonto, P2,633; Paulino Bueno, P579; Telesfora Profeta, P1,528; Claro Buela, P693; Mariano Bunao, P7,715; Mariano Bradecina, P3,127; Pablo Bringuela, P736; Feliciano Belgar, P1,211; Francisco Biblianeas, P464; Domingo Bongay, P2,506; Romualdo Balingbing, P1,163; Canuto Bonrao, P828; Rafael Bugñalbal, P1,177; Leon Bivaro, P1,718; Agapito Boton, P1,449; Jose Bobiles, P1,077; Martin Buela, P852; Geronimo Binaday, P535; Felix Boticario, P2,680; Maximo Boticario, P1,315.50; Anselmo Boticario, P2,929; Juan Bonita, P2,188; Luis Bosotros, P1,245; Francisco Buendia, P3,000; Hermenegildo Bola, P426; Francisco Butial, P443; Ciriaco Bulala, P950; Juan Bonaobra, P2,936; Joaquin Borleo, P1,433; Melquiades Blanquesa, P832; Emeterio Campit, P818; Pacifico Cañoso, P406; Segundo Boticario, P777; Pablo Bosio, P500; Josefa Bungay, P1,072; Apolonio Buasan, P2,147; Emeterio Buising, P520; Marcelo Brondial, P978; Mariano Belenso, P2,840; Dionisio Coruel, P1,460; Froilan Bondal, P3,262; Basilio Bombales, P664; Tomas Bosque, P1,159; Ambrosio Cal, P261; Toribio canon, P391; Fausto Buesa, P412; Silvino Brondial, P1,061.50; Mariano Brondial, P743; Mateo Coruel, P541; Pedro Calising, P1,153; Santiago Bunao, P1,171; Pedro Belenso, P486; Fruto Bragais, P770.50; Francisco Cañon, P544; Natalio Cañon, P660; Esteban Bradecina, P761; Roman Bonto, P526.50; Adriano Bordeos, P1,715; Simeon Blanquesa, P2,021.50; Andres Bringuela, P287.50; Esteban Bugñal-bal, P1,853; Leoncio Buela, P1,403.50; Basilio Cañon, P207; Victor Bombales, P111.50; Mateo Bringuela, P155;

Anastacio Buenviaje, P548. 50; Mariano Biron, P1,184; Simeon Biron, P1,110; Ciriaco Bongay, P363; Inocencio Brosola, P230; Micael Ribandor, P445; Irineo Bonagua, P3,277; Esteban Bonaobra, P660; Tomas Bocito, P145; Victoriano Bongay, P428; Modesto Brutas, P116; Mariano brutas, P581; Cenon Brondial, P882; Claro Begar, P347; Pedro Coruel, P1,137; Tomas Bueno, P1,965; Estanislao Boticario, P313; Laurencio Bosque, P509; Simeona Bongay, P4,709; Ambrosio Borcer, P603; Juan Burac, P557; Antonio Boticario, P215; Meliton Belenso, P332.50; Victor Belenso, P1,384; Hermogenes Cal, P382; Sixto Brutas, P466; Macario Buico, P622; Isidoro Belangel, P2,677; Sergio Buisa, P581.50; Juan Bungay, P624; Victor Bungay, P740; Estanislao Bonaobra, P584; Ana Bonaobra, P317; Esteban Bungay, P1,763. 50; Fortunato Buela, P1,528; Alvaro Boticario, P4,155; Mariano Briquillo, P468; Juan Bolo, P1,655; Isabelo Biblieaneas, P1,955; Arcadio Buela, P544; Gregorio Buragay, P1,184; Meliton Buela, P2,624; Victor Malagueño, P2,876; Timoteo Berlon, P746; Basilio Bonitis, P410; Faustino burce, P588; Vicente Celon, P1,333; Doroteo Belangel, P481; Alejandro Bercer, P1,386; Agaton Bercer, P761; Alberto Bonto, P601; Doroteo Boqueo, P2,799; Agapito Belses, P1,429; Cayetano Buising, P307.50; Teodorico Brutas, P175; Luis Buncay, P3,385; Juan Bento, P2,089; Natalio Canon, P435; Francisco Buelba, P408; Apolonio Buasan, P271; Jose Blando, P415; and Pedro Boticario, P2,359.

That each coconut palm was worth P5; each cacao, P10; each anahao, P1; each nipa, P1; each hectare of abaca, P100; each hectare of sugarcane, P100; each banana stalk, 50 centavos; each caragomoy stalk, P1; eachgallang stalk, 50 centavos; each lemon tree, P1; each coffee plant, P5; and each clump of bamboo, P2; that the defendant, Villanueva, knowing that he was he owner of the land in question, did, with notoriously bad faith tolerate and allow each and all of the plaintiffs to continue to make their sowings, plantings, buildings, and other improvements in order that when terminated, he might appropriate the same to himself, to the plaintiff's prejudice; that the latter, by reason of such bad faith on the part of the defendant were jointly injured to the amount of P200,000; that he (counsel aforesaid) had set forth in the amended complaint that in the preceding one material errors were committed with respect to the names of some of the plaintiffs, though without specifying what they were; that, subsequent to the said complaint, Villanueva took possession of the land in litigation under the authority of a judicial order given in a final judgment, as a result of which the plaintiffs were ousted from the land and the defendant, Villanueva, appropriated to himself all the sowings, plantings, houses and other improvements, the subject matter of this suit; that the defendant had not paid the plaintiffs the value of the said sowings, plantings, houses, and other improvements, which were worth P470,147, and much less the losses and damages afore-mentioned. Counsel therefore prayed that judgment be rendered by sentencing the defendant, Villanueva, to pay to the plaintiffs the sum of P470,147, and, in addition thereto, P200,000, as losses and damages, and the costs of the case.

The defendant, after the demurrer filed by him in answer to the amended complaint had been sustained, denied each and all of the allegations of the complaint in so far as they were not expressly and specifically admitted in his answer, and set forth that he admitted that some of the plaintiffs had been in possession of the land concerned and were residents of the Islands of San Miguel, but denied that they all were such and also the truth of the avernments or allegations contained in the other paragraphs of the complaint, and, as a special defense, set forth that some of the plaintiffs had expressly refused to maintain the complaint in the present case; that the greater part of the alleged sowings and plantings were spontaneous and natural products of the land owned by the defendant; that the plaintiffs acted in bad faith and therefore were not entitled to any indemnity, for the possession which they claimed to hold over certain proportions of the land in question was of precarious nature, since they had no bona fide just title and a sufficient length of time had not yet elapsed to enable them to acquire the property; and that the subject of this suit was one that had already been tried in civil cases Nos. 29 and 33, as shown by Exhibits A and B. As a cross complaint and counterclaim he alleged that the plaintiffs, knowing that the defendant Villanueva, was the owner of, and had obtained title from the state to, the land in question, did, in 1902 and against his will, enter thereon, and possessed themselves of and usufructed the same, in bad faith, until they were ousted by the sheriff in 1908 acting under the authority of a judicial order contained in a final judgment rendered in the said cases, Nos. 29 and 33; that the defendant was by such trespass caused losses and damages through the non-collection of the rents and products of said land during the time of its detention, at the rate of 50 centavos conant, per month — the reasonable rental value of each hectare occupied by each one of the plaintiffs from the year 1892 until they were ousted in 1908; that the plaintiffs, being aware as they were of the defendant's right and of the title he held, prevented him from the enjoyment of the land and compelled him to employ the services of attorneys, who were required in the Court of First Instance and in the Supreme Court, thereby occasioning him losses and damages, in addition to other expenses, losses and damages, in addition to other expenses, besides loss of time and prevention from cultivating the land and deriving profit therefrom, and that such expenses, losses and damages amounted to P20,000. He therefore prayed that the defendant be absolved from the complaint and that the plaintiff be sentenced: (1) To pay P20,000; (2) to pay, each of them, 50 centavos per month for each hectare of land occupied by each of them from the year 1892 until they were ousted in 1908; (3) to keep perpetual silence with regard to the land in question, its sowings, plantings, and other improvements; and (4) to pay the costs of the trial.

Counsel for the plaintiff, after entering an exception to the ruling admitting the defendant's cross complaint, presented a written answer to the special defense and to the cross complaint and counterclaim, and set forth that he denied each and all of the allegations contained in the special defense and in the so-called cross complaint and counterclaim, in each and all of their parts, and prayed that the plaintiffs be absolved from the said cross complaint and counterclaim.

By a written motion of May 20, 1909, counsel for the plaintiffs stated that, for the purpose of the best understanding and most correct judgment of the facts in this case and to avoid confusion, he considered it necessary and expedient that the court appoint a commission composed of three impartial persons who should proceed to count the houses, sowings and plantings, the subject matter of the plaintiff's claim, including those of them that had disappeared, if any such there were and could be determined, and suggested that said commission could, should the court so order, count what pertained individually to each plaintiff, or merely the total number of such improvements, for it was necessary that the court should have an inspection made of the said houses, sowings and plantings as soon as practicable, in view of the fact that counsel had been informed that the defendant was causing them to disappear; that, should the court wish to consider the plaintiffs as one single person, they would waive their right to be considered individually and separately, for the purpose of such judgment as might be rendered in their behalf and the counting of the houses, sowings and plantings aforementioned, for they had agreed that, as soon as a favorable judgment should be rendered, they would divide among themselves the amount awarded them thereby; in a manner proportionate to their respective claims; and that, should the defendant object to the appointment of the said commission on account of expenses and the court decide that he could not rightfully be compelled to pay them, the plaintiffs would bind themselves to reimburse the same as costs upon the defeated party. He therefore prayed that the court appoint the said commissioners and have the inspection made, without awaiting the termination of the taking of evidence.

By an order of May 24 of the same year, 1909, provision was made among others for the appointment of two special commissioners, one by the plaintiffs and the other by the defendant, for the purpose of inspecting the 1,300 hectares of land on the Island of San Miguel and ascertaining and examining facts relative thereto, in order to enable them to use the same in case they should testify as witnesses in this suit, but without authority to present any report whatever as to the result of such inspection.

On page 62 of the bill of exceptions is found an agreement made by the attorneys for the litigants, in regard to the following points: That they admitted that the commission appointed for the taking of evidence might consider all the plaintiffs who had not testified up to date as if they had been presented as witnesses in this suit, with the exception of those in Albay, 35 in number, mentioned by name, who would be presented later, counsel for the defendant assenting that the plaintiffs not excepted should be deemed to have testified; that they had houses, sowings and plantings on the Islands of San Miguel; that the improvements specified in the complaint were those there made since 1891 and prior to 1906; that each witness should answer the following question; "Who did you believe was the owner of the land occupied by you on the Island of San Miguel, at the time that you built your house and made the sowings and plantings now claimed by you in the complaint?"; that during the time that they were building their houses, sowing, and planting, they were not obliged to suspend their work by Mariano Villanueva or by an other person in his name; that counsel for the defendant admitted that the said plaintiffs those whose testimony was, by this agreement, to be considered as valid, might testify with regard to the value and number of their respective houses, sowings and plantings, specified in the complaint, and that such testimony should be given the same weight as if it had been taken before the commissioner in open court, should form an integral part of the record in this case and should be considered as having been given by the said plaintiffs individually or separately, but that this agreement was not to be interpreted in the sense that the defendant must admit the facts contained in such testimony. This agreement was approved by the commissioner, Luis Orteza.

After hearing of the case and introduction of evidence by the parties, the court, on January 28, 1910, rendered the judgment aforementioned, exception to which was taken by counsel for the plaintiffs, who filed a written motion for a new trial. This motion was overruled by an order of February 26, 1910, excepted to by plaintiff's counsel, and, an appropriate bill of exception having been presented, the same was approved and forwarded to the clerk of this court.

In March, 1902, case No. 29 was commenced in the Court of First Instance of Albay through a complaint for the recovery of possession made by Mariano P. Villanueva against Miguel Berses and nine other parties as the usurpers of a tract of land of the plaintiff's ownership situated on the Island of San Miguel. Before the complaint was answered the judge, by an order of April 18, 1903, directed that the case be considered with another in the same court, designated under No. 33 and prosecuted by the same plaintiff against Alejandro Brusola and three others, also occupants of the said land, for the same purpose of recovering possession of the property. Both cases being thus consolidated, their prosecution was continued as though they were a single one, at the instance of the plaintiff, Mariano P. Villanueva, and against the 14 hectares.

Later, by a motion of February 11, 1905, the attorney for the defendants requested the court to rule that the parties named in the complaint as the defendants, besides representing themselves, also represented the other persons interested in the case, under the denomination of "inhabitants of the Island of San Miguel," pursuant to section 118 of the Code of Civil Procedure, and alleged that the interested parties were not only those names appeared in the complaint, but also very many others who might number more than 3,000 persons, inhabitants, nearly all of them, of the said island, for both the former and the latter had and still had a common and general interest in the pending a suit as a matter of a concern of all. The judge, therefore, by an order of February 13 of the same year, directed that "under the denomination of 'and other inhabitants of the Island of San

Miguel, Tabaco, Albay, P. I.,' the persons who had and have an interest in the 1,300 hectares of land in question, situated on the said island, shall be includes as defendants."

The trial being had in all its proceedings, with the attendance of the Attorney-General in behalf of the Government of the United States which as a third party opposed the plaintiff's claim, and after the production of evidence by the parties, the court, on December 3, 1906, rendered judgment by finding that the land sought to be recovered belonged to the plaintiff, Villanueva, ordered the defendants to deliver to him the possession of the same, and absolved the plaintiff from the intervenor's complaint, with the costs equally upon the defendants and the intervener. Counsel for the defendants appealed from this judgment and the appeal having been brought in second instance before this court, was affirmed by the decision of March 25, 1908.

In compliance with a writ addressed to the sheriff of the province and his deputies, proceedings were taken for the execution of the said final judgment, and among other mandates, the defendants were ordered to deliver the possession of the land in litigation to the plaintiff, Mariano Villanueva, and to pay the costs; and, although it is alleged that all those who now appear as the plaintiffs in this case were ousted from the land, the proceedings had in execution show that notification was served on only 8 of the 14 persons expressly sued and whose names appear in the complaints of the previous consolidated cases Nos. 29 and 33, six of whom apparently were neither notified nor warned to vacate their respective lands; but, on the other hand, the record shows that many who do not appear expressly as defendants in the said consolidated cases were so notified, and, in the new complaint afterwards filed by Miguel Berses and 318 others claim to be injured — a complaint which initiated this case, No. 943 of the court of Albay and No. 7309 of the calendar of the Supreme Court — it is alleged that all the 319 plaintiffs were ousted from the land recovered by Mariano P. Villanueva, now the defendant in the present case.

On the hypothesis, the, that all the land comprising the 1,300 hectares, the subject matter of the action for recovery, was entitled released and vacated by its deforciants and placed at the disposal of Mariano P. Villanueva, the owner thereof recognized as such by final judgment of the courts, it is to be presumed that all the occupants of the said land were ejected and expelled therefrom, not only the 14 defendants in the action for recovery, but also the 305 usurpers of the land sought to be recovered by Villanueva as the owner thereof, notwithstanding that these 305 occupants of the property were not expressly sued in the actin aforementioned nor was judgment rendered against them.

So that, of the 319 persons figure in the present case as plaintiff and demand indemnity for losses and damages and for the value of the improvements which they each had made on their respective portions of the land in question held by them up to the date when they were ousted therefrom, only 14 of them were sued by Mariano P. Villanueva through the action for recovery brought in the previous case and the other 305 were not heard therein, notwithstanding which they were ousted and compelled to vacate their respective lands by virtue of the aforesaid judgment which ordered that all the land be restored to its recognized owner, M. P. Villanueva.

Both in the judgment appealed from and in that rendered in the previous action for recovery, it was held that, in accordance with the evidence introduced in the one case and in the other, the 14 defendants in the first one were mere deforciants and possessors in bad faith of the respective portions of the land they were occupying comprised within the property belonging to the present defendant, Villanueva, inasmuch as not only those 14 defendants, but also the rest of the occupants of the land recovered in the previous suit, were well aware that the whole of the land in question, comprising an area of 1,300 hectares belonged to the then plaintiff, Mariano P. Villanueva, who, since November 1, 1890, had held title thereto by composition with the state, which title was registered on June 13, 1891, while the 14 defendants, and doubtless the rest of the occupants of the land concerned in that suit, were absolutely destitute of any title such as might in any manner legalize and justify the possession or tenancy which they had been enjoying of their respective portions of the said land.

The Civil Code prescribes as follows:

ART. 363. He who builds, plants, or sows in bad faith on another's land losses what he has built, planted, or sown, without right to indemnity.

ART. 363. The owner of the land on which anyone has built, planted, or sown in bad faith may demand the demolition of the work or the removal of the plaintiff or sowing and the restoring of everything to its original condition at the expense of the person who built, planted, or sowed.

ART. 433. Any person who is not aware that there is in his title or in the manner of acquiring it any flaw invalidating the same shall be considered a possessor in good faith.

Possessors aware thereof are considered possessor in bad faith.

If the plaintiff had already been in possession of the land before the issuance of the title to the defendant, Villanueva, in November, 1890, they would, through the means of the notices and publications made in the place where the lands is situated and of its measurements and survey, have had an opportunity to object during the course of the proceedings and present adverse claims in defense of their rights and interests.

The claim being restricted to improvements and to losses and damages occasioned subsequent to the grant to the defendant of the adjustment title proving his ownership of the said land, and after the termination of the administration proceedings (in which it is presumed all the legal formalities were complied with and that the land, the composition of which was sought, was uncultivated royal land), and upon the issuance of the proper title to Mariano P. Villanueva, in November, 1890, he became the sole proprietor and tenant as owner of such land granted by the state through adjustment, inasmuch as the Government, in granting the ownership title to the said land, did so with the understanding that the latter was unappropriated and not in the legal possession of anyone.

Aside from the foregoing, there arise the question brought up by the defendant and decided affirmatively in the judgment appealed from, to wit, whether the claim for the payment of the improvements and the indemnity for losses and damages should have been the subject of a counterclaim and have been made during the previous suit brought for the recovery of the land on which such improvements were effected and the losses and damages were suffered by the plaintiffs, as by them alleged.

The first part of section 97 of the Code of Procedure in Civil Actions provides:

Effect of omission to set up counterclaim. — If the right out of which the counterclaim, arises exists at the time of the commencement of the action and arises out of the transaction set forth in the complaint as the foundation of the plaintiff's claim, or is necessarily connected with the subject of the action, neither the defendant nor his assignee can afterwards maintain an action against the plaintiff therefor, if the defendant omits to set up a counterclaim for the same.

In view of the terns and sense of the provisions just above quoted, it is undeniable and to be understood of course that the right of action and other rights alleged by the plaintiff in this suit existed on the date when Villanueva, now the defendant, filed his complaint for the recovery of the land on which the plaintiffs allege they made the improvements, the value of which they claim, and suffered the losses and damages occasioned them; for, since the action brought by Villanueva had for its object the recovery of the land wrongfully detained by the plaintiffs, on the ground that he was the owner and proprietor thereof, and the 14 plaintiffs, the defendants in the previous suit, were unable to allege or present any title whatever showing that they had a better right of possession such as might outweight and invalidate the composition title obtained by Villanueva for the said land, and, furthermore, because of the statements and avernments made by the latter in his complaint for recovery, the defendants in that action, plaintiffs herein, ought to have understood from the beginning that they would very likely be defeated in the suit, as occurred, and for this reason they should have set up a counterclaim in that case for the value of the improvements and the amount of the losses and damages demanded herein, inasmuch as such improvements and indemnity were necessarily connected with the suit for the restitution or recovery of the land claimed to have been improved, and with the results of the execution of the judgment awarding that recovery.

The 14 plaintiffs, the defendants in that previous suit, did not duly present the proper counterclaim, notwithstanding that, in answering the complaint in the action for recovery, they alleged that the value of the lands they possessed, owing to the improvements made by them thereon by plowing and cultivation, amounted to P300,000. Pursuant to the specific provisions of the section aforecited, this omission on the part of the plaintiffs bars them from presenting any claim whatever against the defendant from improvements.

With respect to the 305 persons, also plaintiffs in this case and who were not expressly sued in the previous one, Nos. 29 and 33 consolidated, relative to the recovery of the land owner by the herein defendant, Mariano P. Villanueva, and in which judgment has already been rendered and executed, although they were in the same condition of possessors in bad faith as the other 14 plaintiffs who were the sole defendants in that previous suit, yet, since these 305 deforciants of the land in litigation were not cited or summoned to appear in the said suit, the final judgment rendered therein could produce no legal effect whatever on them nor affect those who were not in due manner actually cited or summoned to appear in that suit prosecuted through the action for recovery brought by the owner of the land, Mariano P. Villanueva, nor were they true parties defendant therein; therefore, in executing the judgment of recovery awarded against those 305 persons who legally were not parties defeated at suit, they were wrongly divested of the possession of their respective portions of land without due process of law, inasmuch as the case prosecuted against the 14 defendants and the judgment rendered therein awarding the recovery was not had against the said 305 persons, herein plaintiffs, who notwithstanding were ousted from and unlawfully divested of the property which they respectively held, even though as usurpers, without proper trial and judgment and without observance of the legal formalities established by the procedural law.

Section 114 of the Code of Civil Procedure, which treats of parties to actions, prescribes as follows:

Every action must be prosecuted in the name of the real party in interest… all persons having an interest in the subject of the action and in obtaining the relief demanded shall be joined as plaintiffs.

Any person should be made a defendant who has or claims an interest in the controversy or the subject matter thereof adverse to the plaintiff, or who is necessary party to a complete determination or settlement of the questions involved therein.

If any person having an interest in the subject of the action, and in obtaining the relief demanded refuses to join as plaintiff with those having alike interest, he may be made a defendant, the fact of his interest and refusal to join being stated in the complaint.

In the document presented in evidence and found on page 95 of the first set of records in Case No. 29 of the court of Albay, the names of Miguel Berses, Saturnino Bon, Leon

Buison, Basilio Buela, Alejandro Bogñalos, Idelfonso Buera, Vicente Bolga, Jacinto Brotas, Alberto Beniste, Tomas Berlon, Alejandro Brusola, Fabian Bonagua, Mariano Bonagua, and Agustin Bonagua, appear as the sole defendants in that suit and it was alleged therein by their counsel that both they and others not mentioned in the record had a common and general interest in the case, and that it was possible for them all to appear at the trial. He therefore requested the court to rule that the defendants named in the complaint represented not only themselves, but also the rest of the parties interested in the suit, under the denomination of "inhabitants of the Island of San Miguel," in accordance with the provision of section 118 of the Code of Civil Procedure.

Notwithstanding that the said defendants' counsel did not state that all the inhabitants of the Island of San Miguel held in common and pro indiviso all or a part of the land claimed by its owner, Villanueva, the court, by an order of February 13, granted the motion and directed that such persons as had and might have an interest in the 1,300 hectares in question should be included in the case under the denomination of "and other inhabitants of the Island of San Miguel, Tabaco, Albay," and this, despite the fact that it was to be presumed that each one of the 319 occupants of the property held separately his respective portion of land independently of the rest, so that they did not have a common interest, but a separate and distinct one with respect to each parcel of land held.

This ruling is undoubtedly on the provisions of the section aforecited, No. 118 of the Code of Civil Procedure, invoked by counsel for the said 14 defendants in that terminated suit; but this court does not agree nor can it accept the judicial criterion which determined the ruling above mentioned, since the provisions of the law refer to cases where a considerable number of persons have a common and general interest in a specific thing and in the trial relating thereto it is impracticable to bring them all before the court. The provisions of section 118 above mentioned are not applicable to a case where each of the persons who should be summoned as defendants in an action brought by a single plaintiff has only a special or particular interest in a specific thing completely different from another thing in which another of the defendants has a like interest, although each of them has the same or analogous reasons and is able to allege the same grounds to impugn the complaint wherein claim is made for the restitution or recovery of all the parts of a property.

Each on of the 319 defendants in the said action, No. 29, prosecuted by Mariano P. Villanueva, was in possession of a parcel or portion of the land comprised within the metes and bounds of the 1,300 hectares of land acquired by the plaintiff, Villanueva, under a composition title with the state. Each on of them, according to the evidence taken in that suit, was a usurper of, or mere trespasser on, the respective portion of land held by him, and inasmuch as none could prove this just title under which he claimed and all of them were in possession with the purpose of appropriating to themselves the respective portions of land occupied by them individually, consequently the all had the same status with respect to the action for recovery brought by the sole owner of the land. But it is no less true that each one of the said 319 defendants held, on the date of the complaint for recovery, a parcel of portion of land completely distinct from the parcel or portion held respectively by each of the 318 other defendants, and each of them, at the commencement of the action, might have alleged a right or special ground which the others could not plead or did not have. The 14 persons who were summoned to appear at court and were defeated in the suit relative to the possession of their respective portions of land might have been able to allege grounds and reasons completely distinct from these which might have been alleged by the other 305 parties who were not summoned and were afterwards, as a result of the final judgment rendered against the sole 14 defendants, ousted from the respective portions of the land they were holding. Some of them might have alleged ordinary or extraordinary prescription, while others perhaps could have shown no right except such as derives from mere possession without title whatsoever.

Furthermore, the said 319 persons, the plaintiffs in this case, were not coheirs or co-owners of anything held in common among them, nor did they possess jointly and pro indigos the 1,300 hectares of land of the Island of San Miguel, but each one of them separately held this respective portion of land each one was sued for the restitution of what he was wrongfully withholding from its rightful owner, according to the demand made by the latter solely against 14 of them. Each one, in a different manner, might have alleged and proved his respective right in the distinct portion occupied him. Therefore it may not be averred that they all had an identical interest and based their possession on precisely the same grounds, for each one might have had distinct interest and rights from those of the rest and each one on the 305 persons who were not parties to the suit might perhaps have alleged and shown better proof then that adduced by the 14 defendants who were defeated in that action concerning the respective portion of land which they each occupied.

Considering, then, that the aforecited provisions of section 118 of the Code of Civil Procedure are not applicable to the present case, as they relate to a common and general interest in single specific things and not to complex and distinct ones, and that, for the reasons aforestated, it was improper to have considered as defendants the 305 persons who were not summoned and did not intervene as parties in the said case No. 29, the final judgment therein rendered could not legally have been executed against the said 305, and therefore, by their being expelled from the tenancy of their respective lands by virtue of such judgment which in no wise could affect them, they were unlawfully despoiled of their possession. Consequently though they are not entitled to lay any claim for improvements made without good faith on the respective parcels of lands they occupied, they have, however, an incontestable right to indemnity for the damages occasioned them as a result of the violent dispossession to which they were subjected in being ousted without previous trial from the respective portions of land they were occupying.

The records dos not show, however, the amount and importance of the damages suffered by each of the said 305 persons, for by the evidence adduced in this case it has neither been proven nor shown what kind of damages were occasioned to them by the execution of the said judgment ordering the restitution of the land sought to be recovered, nor what was the amount of such damages with respect to each one of the interested parties. It is therefore expedient for the purpose of justice that a rehearing be had and new evidence taken therein conducive to prove the said two points in relation to each one of the plaintiffs.

With respect to the counterclaim made by the defendant and disallowed in the judgment appealed from, since the latter entered no exception to such absolutory finding of the trial court, no cognizance thereof can be taken by us.

For the foregoing reasons, whereby the errors assigned to the judgment appealed from are deemed to have been refuted, it is proper to of from the said judgment, as we do hereby, with respect to the aforenamed 14 defendants concerned in the said case, Nos. 29 and 33 consolidated, each of whom shall pay one of the 319 parts into which the costs of both instances are considered to be divided; and the said judgment is reversed as regards that other 305 plaintiffs, whose names appear in the complaint. The record shall be remanded to the court of its origin, accompanied by a certified copy of this decision, in order that it may proceed to reopen the case with respect to the aforesaid 305 plaintiffs who were not parties defendant in the previous one, No. 29, and, after amendment of the complaint with respect to the damages that may have been occasioned by the execution of the judgment of recovery in so far as they were thereby affected, to taken evidence relevant to the points above specified, and finally to render such judgment as the law and the evidence require. So ordered.

Arellano, C.J., Johnson and Carson, JJ., concur.

Separate Opinions

MORELAND, J., concurring:

With respect to the plaintiffs, except those designated as "the fourteen," the judgment should be set aside and the cause returned for trial upon the merits."

The viciousness and fierceness of the *curse* given by the displaced people of San Miguel and their descendants made the descendants of Mariano (I) reeling in apprehension and anxiety. Though most of them do not profess to be superstitious, every time something terrible happens to any member of the Villanueva clan, they remember and relate it to the curse. They count back generations and let out a sigh of relief when they find out that they no longer belong to that cursed generation of Villanueva.

The anger and resentment of the displaced people and their descendants never abated. To them the court decision that they were trespassers was irrelevant. Descendants of Mariano (I) continually encountered hostile people from the Island for more than one hundred years. It would not be a surprise if the hostilities will likely continue to the 21th century.

Most of the succeeding generations that inhabited the Island of San Miguel were probably not aware of the claim, counterclaim and the final decision of the Court regarding the Island of San Miguel that took place before Mariano P. Villanueva (I) sold the island to an American, named Taylor. The following recorded interview of Mrs. Villar supports the unfamiliarity of the people of San Miguel of the court case.

In Fr. O'Brien , *Historical and Cultural Heritage of the Bicol People*, under the heading: ***Tabaco*** by Nilo Ezequiel and Nathaniel Simbahon ' 67; paragraph 27; titled ***San Miguel Island,*** a lady by the name of Pomposa Loyola Vda. De Villar, age 75 and her daughter gave this account as recorded and written down by the aforementioned authors:[30]

"In 1905 when she was only fourteen, a land grabber, a certain Mariano Villanueva, took over the island, which up until then had been held as a common property, and drove off all the farmers there. The Loyola family then settled in Tabaco on a piece of land given by Villanueva. They were about the only family to receive compensation. After some time Villanueva sold his land for 150,000 pesos (?) to a Mr. Robertson, (?) an American. He in turn after some years, sold it to a Mr. Gancayco. These owners covered the island with coconut trees and then a strange thing happened there. In 1926, the dreaded disease (Cadang-Cadang?) *of the coconut industry made it first appearance right on the San Miguel Island! From here it has been spreading further north and south and it is now threatening the Tagalog provinces."*

Maybe, Mrs. Villar and probably most of the inhabitants of San Miguel Island were not aware of the litigation and the final judgement of the Philippine Supreme court in favor of Mariano P. Villanueva in the case of the tenants of San Miguel vs. Mariano P. Villanueva.

The main reason for selling the San Miguel Island to Mr. Taylor, (Mrs. Villar said Mr. Robertson) was due to his marital problem. He was estranged from his wife. The estrangement came about when he wanted to bring his mistress and their children to the ancestral home to live with Teodora and their legitimate children. Teodora, packed up and moved to their other house near the Tabaco church. It was the house that was later purchased and converted to Daniel B. Peña Memorial High School.

Nine of the ten children sided with their mother. Only Isidora sided with her father. After the break-up, Mariano P. (I) enraged that his mistress and his four children were not accepted by the family sold the ancestral house to Smith Bell & Co., and the island of San Miguel was sold to Mr.Taylor.[31] He gave his wife a small amount of allowance through his administrator, Mr. Enrique V. Kare. It was known that she had to beg Mr. Kare for an increase in her allowance.[32]

Nobody really knows how much money Mariano got from the sale of these properties although, Mrs. Pompona Loyola Villar said San Miguel Island was sold for P150,000.00 pesos[33] Mrs. Villar did not cite where she got the amount of sale.

Mariano P. Villanueva (I) bought four big houses, each one occupying one block of land in Manila and gave them to the four illegitimate children. After giving some jewelry to Isidora, he put the rest in Monte de Piedad.[34] There was a rumor that out of anger he threw his gold coins into the sea between San Miguel and Tabaco. But most of the members of the family believed that Isidora got them all. Mariano lived with his illegitimate children in Manila until he died and was buried in Manila.

The following is the full transcript of the divorce papers filed by Teodora Arana in 1910 and was argued in court on November 9, 1915.[35] The court ruled against her citing that she tolerated his philandering throughout their marriage.

239 U.S. 293

36 S.Ct. 109

60 L.Ed. 293

TEODORA ARANA DE VILLANUEVA, Appt.,
v.
MARIANO P. VILLANUEVA.

No. 65.

Argued November 9, 1915.

Decided December 6, 1915.

Mr. C. W. O'Brien for appellant.

Messrs. Howard Thayer Kingsbury and Frederic R. Coudert for appellee.

Mr. Chief Justice White delivered the opinion of the court:

1

The decree which the appellant seeks to reverse affirmed one rendered by the court of first instance, rejecting her demand for a divorce from her husband and for a liquidation and partition of the property belonging to the legal community which existed between them. at the outset we say that we think there is no foundation for the suggestion that we are without jurisdiction because of the inadequacy of the amount involved, since the complaint by which the suit was begun alleged the existence of such an amount of community property as to give jurisdiction, and because the affidavit filed for the purpose of the appeal also so establishes, there being no countervailing affidavit and nothing in the record to demonstrate to the contrary. De la Rama v. De La Rama, *201 U. S. 303*, 50 L. ed. 765, 26 Sup. Ct. Rep. 485.

2

The complaint for divorce and liquidation of the community as it was finally amended, which was filed in 1910, alleged the marriage of the parties in 1867 and the birth of ten children, nine of whom were alive and of age and one of whom was dead, leaving surviving issue. As a basis for the divorce prayed various acts of adultery by the defendant were charged, extending over a period of forty-two years; that is, from 1868, shortly after the marriage, until the bringing of the suit in 1910. The facts thus charged embraced six periods: that first, from 1868 until the filing of the suit with a named person, from which relation it was alleged there had been begotten five children, four of whom were alive and bore their father's surname; the second, with another named person during 1889 and 1890, from which relation there was begotten a daughter who likewise bore her father's surname; the third, with a named person during the year 1891; the fourth with a name person from 1892 until the time the suit was commenced, from which relation it was alleged children also were begotten; the fifth, with a named person during the years 1901 and 1902; and the sixth, with a named person during the years 1903 and 1904. The answer set up a general denial, a special defense that if the acts of adultery alleged were found to have been committed, they were done with the knowledge of the complainant, who had condoned them, and, moreover, that the action was prescribed.

3

After full hearing the court of first instance found that the defendant had been guilty of adultery with the person named in the complaint in the first period during the years from 1868 until 1900, but that there was no proof of any such adultery having been committed by him with the person named for the ten years preceding the suit, that is, from 1900 to 1910. The court also found that it was established that the defendant had adulterous relations with the person named during the second period, that is, from 1889 to 1890, and that from such relations, as alleged, a daughter named Maria was begotten, but that the relations had ceased years before the bringing of the suit, since the woman named had died long before at a period fixed approximately as the time of the beginning of the American occupation of the islands. The court also found that it had been proved that acts of adultery had been committed with the person named during the fourth period, that is, in 1892 and some time thereafter, but it also affirmatively found that all relations between the defendant and the person named in this period had ceased prior to 1900. It was moreover expressly found that there was no proof whatever offered concerning any of the other acts of adultery charged in the complaint.

4

Concerning the first period, the court found that the proof left no doubt that the complainant at an early date became aware of the adulterous relations to which that period related, and although she did so, continued her marital relations with her husband and had condoned his infidelity. Indeed, it was found that forgiveness by the wife was clearly established from the fact that during the ten years which had elapsed before the bringing of the suit and after the illicit relations had ceased, the children begotten of such relation were brought into the household with the consent of the wife, and lived as part of the common family. Applying the law to this condition it was held that the condonement or forgiveness was a complete bar to the suit based upon the acts which had been thus forgiven. So far as concerned the acts of infidelity committed during the second and fourth periods, as stated, although it was found that there was no direct proof that the complainant knew of such wrongs when committed, nevertheless it was held that there was no ground for awarding relief because of such acts irrespective of the question of forgiveness or condonement resulting from the long continuance of the marital relations after such acts had been committed, for the reason that the complainant had expressly declared in testifying that she solely asked relief because of the acts embraced in the first period, and none other,—a situation which, it was held, brought the case directly within the control of Laws 1 and 2, title 9, Partida 4, expressly confining the right to complain of adultery by one of the parties to a marriage to the injured party. And this conclusion was sustained by pointing out that although the complaint for divorce had been sworn to by the complainant, she had in her testimony admitted that she knew nothing of the particular acts embraced in the periods in question, and intended only to sue for those described in the first period; thus, as to such other acts, giving rise to the implication that their averment was the result of the instigation of some person not authorized to act, probably impelled by some interest direct or indirect in the liquidation of the community property which would follow if the prayer of the complainant had been granted.

5

In a careful opinion the court below, reviewing the action of the court of first instance, adopted and reaffirmed in every substantial particular the facts found by that court, and also agreed with the legal conclusions which the court had applied to the facts by it found. In applying the law to the facts it was pointed out that the controlling law was to be found not in the Civil Code, but in the Particas, and it was held that as by provisions of the Partidas which were cited it was expressly provided that condonement or forgiveness of acts of adultery excluded the subsequent right to relief based upon the fact that they had been committed, it followed from the conclusive proof of forgiveness resulting from the facts found that no error had been committed in rejecting the demand for a divorce. In stating the reasons, which led it to this conclusion the mind of the court was principally directed to the acts of infidelity found to have been committed during the first period and the acts by which forgiveness as to them had been indubitably established. But the court, considering the facts found as to the other two periods, without deciding that such acts of infidelity had not been condoned, expressly held that the necessary result of the provisions of the Partidas which had been applied by the lower court, exclusively confining the right to relief for acts of infidelity to the injured spouse, plainly justified the court of first instance in its ruling that the disclaimer of all right to relief as to any acts but those which the complaint alleged were committed during the first period excluded all right to recover for any but those acts, to which the controversy thus became confined.

6

The first two of the nine assignments of error question the finding and ruling of the court concerning the acts committed during the first period and their condonement or forgiveness. The third and fourth assail the correctness of the conclusion concerning the second and fourth periods and the ruling of the court relating to them, based on the disclaimer made by the complainant in her testimony of any right to relief on account of them; and as cognate to this subject, the fifth complains of the action of the court in analyzing the motives which prompted the inclusion in the suit of causes upon which the complainant asserted she did not rely for relief, for the purpose of bringing the case within the rule laid down in Laws 1 and 2, title 9, Partida 4, which both courts applied. The remainder in general terms but assert error committed in the findings and in the law which was applied to them in deciding the cause.

7

Although the arguments pressed at bar to sustain these assignments apparently enlarge them, in substance they add nothing to them, but simply reiterate in changed and more minute forms of statement the grounds of error asserted in the assignments. Under these conditions it is apparent that all the errors relied upon, whether embraced in the assignments or pressed in the argument, considered in their essence, only dispute the correctness of the facts found by both the courts below, and but challenge the accuracy of the principles of the local law which were applied to the facts for the purpose of deciding the cause. Under these circumstances, without noticing more in detail either the assignments or the arguments supporting them, we content ourselves with saying that we are of the opinion, after examining and weighing them all, that they are without merit for the follwing reasons: (a) Because in so far as they dispute the concurrent findings of fact of both the courts below, they entirely fail to give rise to that conviction of clear error which must be entertained in order to authorize a reversal of the findings (Texas & P. R. Co. v. Railroad Commission, *232 U. S. 338*, 58 L. ed. 630, 34 Sup. Ct. Rep. 438; Gilson v. United States, *234 U. S. 380*, 383, 384, 58 L. ed. 1361, 1362, 1363, 34 Sup. Ct. Rep. 778); and (b) because in so far as they challenge the correctness of the application which the courts made of the local law to the facts in deciding the cause, they are totally deficient in that persuasive strength which it is essential they should possess in order to produce the conviction that clear error was committed by the court below, and thus lead us to depart from the principle by which we follow and sustain the local law as applied by the court below unless we are constrained to the contrary by a sense of clear error committed (Ker & Co. v. Couden, *223 U. S. 268*, 279, 56 L. ed. 432, 435, 32 Sup. Ct. Rep. 284; Santa Fe C. R. Co. v. Friday, *232 U. S. 694*, 700, 58 L. ed. 802, 803, 34 Sup. Ct. Rep. 468; Nadal v. May, *233 U. S. 447*, 454, 58 L. ed. 1040, 1041, 34 Sup. *Ct. Rep. 611).*

8

Affirmed.

When Mariano P. (I) died, he was worth P400,000.00 according to Dr. Owen in his book, *Bikol Blend*.[36] His administrator was Enrique V. Kare who put Teodora Arana under a small allowance that she had to *beg* for increase in her allowance.[37] It has been discussed and well known among the Villanuevas that Enrique V. Kare and some of his descendants became very rich for administering the properties of Mariano.[38]

The Coal Mine holdings of the Messrs. Villanueva and Company are as follows:[39]

1. Date of entry: December 21,1893; Name of Mine: **Balerma**; Locality: Pulutan, Isla de Batan; District: Bacon, Province : Sorsogon (Albay); One claim of 150,000 Sq. meters – concession date: August 16, 1895 – First Class

2. Date of entry: December 21,1893; Name of Mine: **Urgera**; Locality: Bencalon, Isla de Batan; District: Bacon; Province: Sorsogon (Albay); One claim of 150,000 Sq. meters – concession date: August 16, 1895 – First Class

3. Date of entry: December 21,1893; Name of Mine: **Ganalda**; Locality: Liguan, Isla de Batan; District of Bacon; Province: Sorsogon (Albay); One claim of 150,000 sq. meters – concession date: August 16,1895 – First Class.

4. Date of entry: January 31,1894; Name of Mine: **Perseverancia**; Locality: Malabog, Isla de Batan; District: Bacon, Province: Sorsogon (Albay); one pertenencia 150,000 Sq. meters – concession date:august 16, 1895 – First Class.

The ten legitimate children of Mariano P. Villanueva (I) and Teodora Arana were very rich in their own right. Most of the sons (including some of the illegitimate sons) were educated abroad and the women were sent to exclusive finishing school in Manila.[40] but there was a reversal of fortune and most of them were financially ruined during the WWII.

1. Pedro A. Villanueva Sr. (I) – the oldest son studied Business in Hong Kong and married his first cousin Quiteria Mabihis Villaueva (I). She was the oldest daughter of Vicente P. Villanueva (I).

2. Francisca A. Villanueva (I) was sent to a finishing school in Manila for women, Centro Escolar de Señoritas, owned by a distant relative of the Villanuevas. She married Santiago Riosa (I), the son of Don Mariano Riosa and Maria Corral.

3. Maria A. Villanueva (II) was also sent to Centro Escolar de Señoritas and married Ignacio Liangco of Malinao.

4. Antonio A. Villanueva (II) - went to study in Spain and married a Spanish lady named Teresita. He never came back to the Philippines.

5. Rafael A. Villanueva (I) - married Mariqueta Zulueta from Guinobatan. There is no record where he had studied.

6. Mariano A. Villanueva (II) - went to Spain to study and married Consuelo Bautista

7. Isidora A. Villanueva (I) also was sent to a finishing school and remained single.

8. Delfin A. Villanueva (I) - married Telesfora Ante and there is no record where he had studied.

9. Candida A. Villanueva (I) also was sent to finishing school and married the Spanish *haciendero* from Tiwi Ramon Morales.

10. Vicente A. Villanueva (II) - went to London to study and married a lady nicknamed "Tinay".

Nobody knows the full name of the mistress of Mariano Sr, (I) that caused the break-up of the Villanueva family. She was, however, called "*Lola Lanyang*".

The known illegitimate children of Mariano (I) with a mistress nicknamed, "*Lola Lanyang*" Quijano, were:

1. Felix Quijano (I) was sent to study in London

2. Melania Quijano (I) married Salcedo

3. Julio Quijano (I) married an orphaned Jew named Rosario Abraham

4. Toribia Quijano married Syqia

Mariano P. (I) with an unknown mistress who died during the American occupation bore his daughter named:

5. Maria (III) Villanueva[41]

Mariano P. (I) fathered a son with Quiteria Buenconsejo

6. Balbino Buenconsejo Villanueva[42]

Genealogical Line of Mariano P. Villanueva (I)

1st Gen: Mariano P. Villanueva (I) – +m. Teodora Arana

2nd Gen:

1. Pedro A. Villanueva Sr. (l) – +m. Quiteria M. Villanueva (I)

2. Francisca A. Villanueva (I) – +m. Santiago Riosa

3. Maria A. Villanueva (Il) – +m. Ignacio Liangco

4. Antonio A. Villanueva (II) – m. Teresita (?)

5. Rafael A. Villanueva (l) – m. Mariqueta Zulueta + +m^2 Flaviana Manjares

6. Mariano A. Villanueva (II) – +m. Consuelo Reanzares Bautista

7. Isidora A. Villanueva (I) - single – **End of line**

8. Delfin A. Villanueva (I) – +m. Telesfora Ante

9. Candida A. Villanueva (I) – +m. Ramon Morales

10. Vicente A. Villanueva (II) – +m Tinay (?)

1st Gen: Mariano P. Villanueva (I) – +n.m. "*Lanyang*" Quijano

2nd Gen:

    11. Felix Quijano (I) – +n.m (?) Maxima Bualoy

    12. Melania Quijano (I)– +m. (?) Salcedo

    13. Julio Quijano (I) – +m. Rosario Abraham

    14. Toribia Quijano +m (?) Siquia

1st Gen: Mariano P. Villanueva (I) – +n.m. unnamed lady

2nd Gen:

    15. Maria Villanueva (III)

!st Gen: Mariano P. Villanueva (I) – +n.m. Quiteria Buenconsejo

2nd Gen:

    16. Balbino B. Villanueva (II) [43]

Notes and Sources

Chapter II

Page 6:

¹ Rios, Angela Villanueva Villanueva Sr. (I); wife of Jesus Salvador Blance Rios Sr.; youngest daughter of Pedro Arana Villanueva Sr. (I) and Quiteria Mabihis Villanueva; granddaughter of Vicente Villanueva (I) and (?) Mabihis; grandaughter Mariano P. Villanueva (I) and Teodora Arana; excerpt from the 1983 interview.

²⁻ **Teodora Arana de Villanueva Appt. vs Mariano P Villanueva,** No. 65 - Court Record on file; paragraph no. 2 and 3. Internet link shared by: Villar, Corina Belle Riosa, daughter of Evelyn de Lejos Riosa and Edwin Villar; granddaughter of Santiago Estevez Riosa Sr. (II) and Muriel Villanueva de Lejos (I); great granddaughter of Magin Villanueva Riosa Sr. (I) and Purificacion Estevez; great granddaughter of Remedios Villanueva Villanueva (I) and Francisco de Lejos; great -great granddaughter of Pedro Arana Viilanueva Sr. (I) and Quiteria Mabihis Villanueva (I); great great granddaughter of Francisca Arana Villanueva (I) and Santiago Riosa (I); great-great great granddaughter of Vicente Villanueva (I) and (?) Mabihis; great great great granddaughter of Mariano P. Villanueva (I) and Teodora Arana.

³ Rios, Angela Villanueva Villanueva Sr. (I); wife of Jesus Salvador Blance Rios Sr.; youngest daughter of Pedro Arana Villanueva Sr. (I) and Quiteria Mabihis Villanueva; granddaughter of Vicente Villanueva (I) and (?) Mabihis; grandaughter Mariano P. Villanueva (I) and Teodora Arana; excerpt from the 1983 interview.

Page 7:

⁴ **Teodora Arana de Villanueva Appt. vs Mariano P Villanueva,** No. 65 - Court Record on file; paragraph no. 2 and 3. Internet link shared by: Villar, Corina Belle Riosa, daughter of Evelyn de Lejos Riosa and Edwin Villar; granddaughter of Santiago Estevez Riosa Sr. (II) and Muriel Villanueva de Lejos (I); great granddaughter of Magin Villanueva Riosa Sr. (I) and Purificacion Estevez; great granddaughter of Remedios Villanueva Villanueva (I) and Francisco de Lejos; great -great granddaughter of Pedro Arana Viilanueva Sr. (I) and Quiteria Mabihis Villanueva (I); great great granddaughter of Francisca Arana Villanueva (I) and Santiago Riosa (I); great-great great granddaughter of Vicente Villanueva (I) and (?) Mabihis; great great great granddaughter of Mariano P. Villanueva (I) and Teodora Arana.

⁵ ibid.

⁶ Ancetry.com

[7] 1887, Catálogo de la Exposicion General de las Islas Filipinas, Celebrada en Madrid, Inaugarada Por M. La Reina Regente. El 30 de Junio de 1887; Madrid: Est. Tipografico de Ricardo Fé, Calle Cedaceros, núm 11, 1887, p. 371.

[8] ibid., p. 472

[9] ibid, p. 526

[10] ibid., p. 546

[11] Torres, Consuelo Bautista Villanueva Jr. (II); wife of Melqueides Torres; youngest daughter of Mariano Arana Villanueva Jr. (II) and Consuelo Bautista Sr.; granddaughter of Mariano P. Villaunueva (I) and Teodora Arana. Excerpt from an interview given in California in the late 1980's.

Page 8:

[12] Morales, Orestes Murillo (I); husband of Dolores Dy Alparce; son of Enrique Villanueva Morales (I) and Trinidad Murillo; grandson of Candida Arana Villanueva (I) and Ramon Morales; great grandson of Mariano P. Villanueva Sr. (I) and Teodora Arana: as told by Fermin Ante Villanueva (I); husband of Anita (¿), and "Laleng" (¿); son of Delfin Arana Villanueva (I) and Pura Ante; grandson of Mariano P. Villanueva (I) and Teodora Arana.

[13] ibid.

[14] Rios, Angela Villanueva Villanueva Sr.(I); wife of Jesus Salvador Blance Rios Sr.; youngest daughter of Pedro Arana Villanueva Sr. (I) and Quiteria Mabihis Villanueva (I); granddaughter of Vicente Villanueva (I) and (?) Mabihis; granddaughter of Mariano P. Villanueva (I) and Teodora Arana. Excerpt from 1983 interview.

[15] Morales, Orestes Murillo (I); husband of Dolores Dy Alparce; son of Enrique Villanueva Morales (I) and Trinidad Murillo; grandson of Candida Arana Villanueva (I) and Ramon Morales; great grandson of Mariano P. Villanueva (I) and Teodora Arana: as told by Fermin Ante Villanueva (I); husband of Anita (¿), and "Laleng" (¿); son of Delfin Arana Villanueva (I) and Pura Ante; grandson of Mariano P. Villanueva (I) and Teodora Arana.

[16] Buenconsejo, Margarita Villanueva de Lejos (I); wife of Anastacio Buenconsejo Sr.; daughter of Remedios Villanueva Villanueva (I) and Francisco de Lejos; granddaughter of Pedro Arana Villanueva Sr. (I) and Quiteria Mabihis Villanueva (I); great - granddaughter of Vicente Villanueva (I) and (?) Mabihis; great granddaughter of Mariano P. Villanueva (I) and Teodora Arana: as told to Lao, Edna de Lejos Buenconsejo; widow of Ricardo Lao; daughter of Margarita Villanueva de Lejos (I) and

Anastacio Buenconsejo Sr.; granddaughter of Remedios Villanueva Villanueva (I) and Francisco de Lejos; great - granddaughter of Pedro Arana Villanueva Sr. (I) and Quiteria Mabihis Villanueva (I); great great - granddaughter of Vicente Villanueva (I) and (?) Mabihis; great great granddaughter of Mariano P. Villanueva (I) and Teodora Arana; long distance telephone interview from Pasay City, Metro Manila, Philippines.

[17] Morales, Orestes Murillo (I); husband of Dolores Dy Alparce; son of Enrique Villanueva Morales (I) and Trinidad Murillo; grandson of Candida Arana Villanueva (I) and Ramon Morales; great grandson of Mariano P. Villanueva (I) and Teodora Arana; as told by Fermin Ante Villanueva (I); husband of Anita (¿), and "Laleng" (¿); son of Delfin Arana Villanueva (I) and Pura Ante; grandson of Mariano P. Villanueva (I) and Teodora Arana.

[18] Common knowledge among older generation

[19] 1953, Bureau of Public School, *History and Cultural Life of the Town of Tabaco and It's Barrios,* Collected in Compliance with Executive Order No. 486, December 7, 1951 as embodied in General Memorandum No. 34, s. 1952.

[20] Owen, Norman G., *The Bikol Blend: Bikolanos and their History*, 1999, Quezon City, Philippines, New Day Publisher, p. 238.

[21] Rios, Angela Villanueva Villanueva Sr.(I); wife of Jesus Salvador Blance Rios Sr.; youngest daughter of Pedro Arana Villanueva Sr. (I) and Quiteria Mabihis Villanueva (I); granddaughter of Vicente Villanueva (I) and (?) Mabihis; granddaughter of Mariano P. Villanueva (I) and Teodora Arana. Excerpt from 1983 interview.

[22] Republic of the Philippines, Supreme Court, Manila, EN BANC, **Miguel Berses and 318 others**, plaintiff appellants vs. **Mariano P. Villanueva**, defendant, appellee, G.R. No. L-7309, October 10 1913. Internet link shared by: Villar, Corina Belle Riosa, daughter of Evelyn de Lejos Riosa and Edwin Villar; granddaughter of Santiago Estevez Riosa Sr. (II) and Muriel Villanueva de Lejos (I); great granddaughter of Magin Villanueva Riosa Sr. (I) and Purificacion Estevez; great granddaughter of Remedios Villanueva Villanueva (I) and Francisco de Lejos; great -great granddaughter of Pedro Arana Viilanueva Sr. (I) and Quiteria Mabihis Villanueva (I); great great granddaughter of Francisca Arana Villanueva (I) and Santiago Riosa; great-great great granddaughter of Vicente Villanueva (I) and (?) Mabihis; great great great granddaughter of Mariano P. Villanueva (I) and Teodora Arana.

[23] Rios, Angela Villanueva Villanueva Sr.(I); wife of Jesus Salvador Blance Rios Sr.; youngest daughter of Pedro Arana Villanueva Sr. (I) and Quiteria Mabihis Villanueva (I); granddaughter of Vicente Villanueva (I) and (?) Mabihis; granddaughter of Mariano P. Villanueva (I) and Teodora Arana. Excerpt from 1983 interview.

Page 9:

[24] Republic of the Philippines, Supreme Court, Manila, EN BANC, **Miguel Berses and 318 others**, plaintiff appellants vs. **Mariano P. Villanueva**, defendant, appellee, G.R. No. L-7309, October 10 1913. Internet link shared by:Villar, Corina Belle Riosa, daughter of Evelyn de Lejos Riosa and Edwin Villar; granddaughter of Santiago Estevez Riosa Sr. (II) and Muriel Villanueva de Lejos (I); great granddaughter of Magin Villanueva Riosa Sr. (I) and Purificacion Estevez; great granddaughter of Remedios Villanueva Villanueva (I) and Francisco de Lejos; great -great granddaughter of Pedro Arana Viilanueva Sr. (I) and Quiteria Mabihis Villanueva (I); great great granddaughter of Francisca Arana Villanueva (I) and Santiago Riosa; great-great great granddaughter of Vicente Villanueva (I) and (?) Mabihis; great great great granddaughter of Mariano P. Villanueva (I) and Teodora Arana.

[25] Forster, Jane Calkins, *The Encomienda System in the Philippine Islands: 1571-1597*, 1956, Master's These, Paper 1010. http://ecommons.luc,edu/luc_theses1010.

[26] Republic of the Philippines, Supreme Court, Manila, EN BANC, **Miguel Berses and 318 others**, plaintiff appellants vs. **Mariano P. Villanueva**, defendant, appellee, G.R. No. L-7309, October 10 1913. Internet link shared by: Villar, Corina Belle Riosa, daughter of Evelyn de Lejos Riosa and Edwin Villar; granddaughter of Santiago Estevez Riosa Sr. (II) and Muriel Villanueva de Lejos (I); great granddaughter of Magin Villanueva Riosa Sr. (I) and Purificacion Estevez; great granddaughter of Remedios Villanueva Villanueva (I) and Francisco de Lejos; great -great granddaughter of Pedro Arana Viilanueva Sr. (I) and Quiteria Mabihis Villanueva (I); great great granddaughter of Francisca Arana Villanueva (I) and Santiago Riosa; great-great great granddaughter of Vicente Villanueva (I) and (?) Mabihis; great great great granddaughter of Mariano P. Villanueva (I) and Teodora Arana.

[27] ibid.

[28] ibid.

Page 13:

[29] ibid

Page 27:

[30] Fr. O'Brien , *Historical and Cultural Heritage of the Bicol People*, under the heading: *Tabaco* by Nilo Ezequiel and Nathaniel Simbahon, ***San Miguel Island*** ' 67; paragraph 27.

Page 28:

[31] Rios, Angela Villanueva Villanueva Sr.(I); wife of Jesus Salvador Blance Rios Sr.; youngest daughter of Pedro Arana Villanueva Sr. (I) and Quiteria Mabihis Villanueva (I); granddaughter of Vicente Villanueva (I) and (?) Mabihis; granddaughter of Mariano P. Villanueva (I) and Teodora Arana. Excerpt from 1983 interview.

[32] Rios, Carlos Manuel Villanueva Sr. (I); husband of Emma Peralta; 5th child and 3rd son of Angela Villanueva Villanueva Sr. (I) and Jesus Salvador Blance Rios Sr.; grandson of Pedro Arana Villanueva Sr. (I) and Quiteria Mabihis Villanueva (I); great grandson of Vicente Villanueva (I) and (?) Mabihis; great grandson of Mariano P. Villanueva (I) and Teodora; as told by: Rios, Angela Villanueva Villanueva Sr.(I); wife of Jesus Salvador Blance Rios Sr.; youngest daughter of Pedro Arana Villanueva Sr. (I) and Quiteria Mabihis Villanueva (I); granddaughter of Vicente Villanueva (I) and (?) Mabihis; granddaughter of Mariano P. Villanueva (I) and Teodora Arana; excerpt from a 2017 telephone conversation.

[33] Fr. O'Brien , *Historical and Cultural Heritage of the Bicol People*, under the heading: ***Tabaco*** by Nilo Ezequiel and Nathaniel Simbahon, **San Miguel Island**' 67; paragraph 27.

[34] Rios, Angela Villanueva Villanueva Sr.(I); wife of Jesus Salvador Blance Rios Sr.; youngest daughter of Pedro Arana Villanueva Sr. (I) and Quiteria Mabihis Villanueva (I); granddaughter of Vicente Villanueva (I) and (?) Mabihis; granddaughter of Mariano P. Villanueva (I) and Teodora Arana. Excerpt from 1983 interview.

[35] *239 U.S. 293, 36 S.Ct. 109, 60 L.Ed. 293,* **TEODORA ARANA DE VILLANUEVA, Appt., v. MARIANO P. VILLANUEVA.** *No. 65.* Argued November 9, 1915. Decided December 6, 1915.Mr. C. W. O'Brien for appellant. Messrs. Howard Thayer Kingsbury and Frederic R. Coudert for appellee.

Page 32:

[36] Owen, Dr. Norman G. , *The Bikol Blend: Bikolanos and their History*, 1999, Quezon City, Philippines, New Day Publisher, p. 238.

[37] Rios, Carlos Manuel Villanueva Sr. (I); husband of Emma Peralta; 5th child and 3rd son of Angela Villanueva Villanueva Sr. (I) and Jesus Salvador Blance Rios Sr.; grandson of Pedro Arana Villanueva Sr. (I) and Quiteria Mabihis Villanueva (I); great grandson of Vicente Villanueva (I) and (?) Mabihis; great grandson of Mariano P. Villanueva (I) and Teodora; as told by: Rios, Angela Villanueva Villanueva Sr.(I); wife of Jesus Salvador Blance Rios Sr.; youngest daughter of Pedro Arana Villanueva Sr. (I) and Quiteria Mabihis Villanueva (I); granddaughter of Vicente Villanueva (I) and (?) Mabihis; granddaughter of Mariano P. Villanueva (I) and Teodora Arana; excerpt from a 2017 telephone conversation.

[38] Rios, Angela Villanueva Villanueva Sr.(I); wife of Jesus Salvador Blance Rios Sr.; youngest daughter of Pedro Arana Villanueva Sr. (I) and Quiteria Mabihis Villanueva (I); granddaughter of Vicente Villanueva (I) and (?) Mabihis; granddaughter of Mariano P. Villanueva (I) and Teodora Arana. Excerpt from 1983 interview.

[39] Burritt, Charles H., First Lieutenant, Eleventh Cavalry, U.S. V., Officer In Charge The Mining Bureau, *The Coal Measure of the Philippines, A Rapid History of the Discovery of Coal in the Archipelago and Subsequent Development, With the Full Texto f the Record of the Macleod Coal Concession in Cebu, or the Uling-Lutac Coal and Railway Concession*, War Department, Division of Insular Affairs, August 1901, Washington: Government Printing Office, p. 253.

Page 33:

[40] Rios, Angela Villanueva Villanueva Sr.(I); wife of Jesus Salvador Blance Rios Sr.; youngest daughter of Pedro Arana Villanueva Sr. (I) and Quiteria Mabihis Villanueva (I); granddaughter of Vicente Villanueva (I) and (?) Mabihis; granddaughter of Mariano P. Villanueva (I) and Teodora Arana. Excerpt from 1983 interview.

Page 34:

[41] Philippine Supreme Court: **Teodora Arana de Villanueva Appt. vs Mariano P Villanueva,** No. 65 - Court Record on file; Internet link shared by: Villar, Corina Belle Riosa, daughter of Evelyn de Lejos Riosa and Edwin Villar; granddaughter of Santiago Estevez Riosa Sr. (II) and Muriel Villanueva de Lejos (I); great granddaughter of Magin Villanueva Riosa Sr. (I) and Purificacion Estevez; great granddaughter of Remedios Villanueva Villanueva (I) and Francisco de Lejos; great -great granddaughter of Pedro Arana Viilanueva Sr. (I) and Quiteria Mabihis Villanueva (I); great great granddaughter of Francisca Arana Villanueva (I) and Santiago Riosa; great-great great granddaughter of Vicente Villanueva (I) and (?) Mabihis; great great great granddaughter of Mariano P. Villanueva (I) and Teodora Arana.

[42] Lianco,Robert Almonte; husband of Jonelyn Gregorio Villanueva who is the daughter of Jose Bobis Villanueva Jr. (II) and Evelyn Gregorio; granddaughter of Jose Villanueva Villanueva Sr. (I) and Eleuteria Bobis; great granddaughter of Pedro Arana Villanueva (I) and Quiteria Mabihis Villanueva (?); great great granddaughter of Vicente Villanueva (I) and (?) Mabihis; great great granddaughter of Mariano P. Villanueva (I) and Teodora Arana. Robert 's lineage shows that he is a relative through marriage and not by blood. The connection had not been properly verified and the Llangco's or Lianco's lineage has very little information.

Page 35:

[43] Ancestry.com

Chapter III

ANNOTATED GENEALOGICAL SUMMARY OF THE VILLANUEVA FAMILY

Note: *In this summary, I have used the abbreviated names of both Vicente P. Villanueva (I) and Mariano P. Villanueva Sr. (I) to designate their genealogical line. The numbers that follow the letters, show to which generations that particular person belongs. Each succeeding generation is separated by a period.*

Example: **VVG-1** *means Vicente Villanueva (Line) First Generation*

MVG-1 *means Mariano Villanueva (Line) First Generation*

VVG-1.1 *means First Generation; first on the 2nd generation under Vicente P.Villanueva "s line.*

MVG-1.1 *means First Generation; first on the 2nd generation under Mariano P. Villanueva's line.*

VMVG-(1&2).(1&1) *means the individuals are first born on the 2nd generation and are first cousins coming from both Vicente's and Mariano's lines.*

VMVG-(1&2). (1&1).1 *means the individual is from both Vicente and Mariano's lines. the parents are first born on their respective generations and are first cousin. the individual is the first on the 3nd generation.*

The Roman numeral that follows each name designates how often that particular name had occurred in the Villanueva's Family Tree. It has nothing to do with succession.

The abbreviation Sr. and Jr. are used regardless of gender. In cases where a person is a Jr. and at the same time he or she had named one of his or her children after him or her will appear as: Jr./ Sr.

+m, or +m^2 - *means married or 2nd marriage, respectively*

+n.m. – *means not married*

+m/s – *means married but separated*

un.or (?) – *means unknown name*

ufn.or (?) - *means unknown first name*

usn. or (?) – *means unknown surname*

FIRST GENERATION OF THE VILLANUEVA FAMILY

          G1   **G2**

VVG.1   **I. VICENTE VILLANUEVA (I)**

CHILDREN OF VICENTE VILLANUEVA (I) WITH +n.m., ufn. (?) MABIHIS of Legaspi

VVG-1.1	1. Quiteria Mabihis Villanueva (I) +m. Pedro Villanueva
VVG-1.2	2. Maria Mabihis Villanueva (I) **End of line**
VVG-1.3	3. Antonio Mabihis Villanueva (I) **End of line**

Notes: Vicente Villanueva lived in Legaspi. He fathered three children[1] with a woman named (?) Mabihis[2]. She is rumored to be the laundrey woman of Vicente.[3] Vicente had a house near the St. George Church at Legaspi[4].

When Mabihis died, he married Tomas who was from Legaspi and was said to be very beautiful. They had a son named Balbino who was also said to be very handsome[5]. Vicente died in 1891 according to Dr. Norman G. Owen. When he died he was supposedly worth P200,000.[6]

Sources: [1&5] Angela Villanueva Rios (I); [2] Muriel Villanueva de Lejos Riosa (I); [3] as told to Manuel Villanueva Rios by the laundry woman of Pedro Arana Villanueva, named Borjal; [4] Corina Belle Riosa Villar; [6] 1999, *Bikol Blend*, Dr. Norman G. Owen, p. 245.

CHILDREN OF VICENTE VILLANUEVA (I) with +m., ufn. (?) TOMAS of Legaspi

VVG-1.4	4. Balbino Tomas Villanueva (I)

MVG.2   **2. MARIANO P. VILLANUEVA (I)**

CHILDREN OF MARIANO P. VILLANUEVA (I) with +m. TEODORA ARANA of Legaspi

MVG-2.1	1. Pedro A. Villanueva Sr. (I) +m. Quiteria M. Villanueva
MVG-2.2	2. Francisca A. Villanueva (I) +m. Santiago Corral Riosa
MVG-2.3	3. Maria A. Villanueva (II) +m. Ignacio Liangco
MVG-2.4	4. Antonio A. Villanueva (II) +m. Teresita (?) (Spain)
MVG-2.5	5. Rafael A. Villanueva (I) +m. Mariquita Zulueta; +m^2. Flaviana Manjares
MVG-2.6	6. Mariano A. Villanueva (II) +m. Consolacion Bautista
MVG-2.7	7. Isidora A. Villanueva (I) single. **End of line**

MVG-2.8   8. Delfin A. Villanueva (I) +m. Telesfora Ante
MVG-2.9   9. Candida A. Villanueva (I) +m. Ramon Morales
MVG-2.10   10. Vicente A. Villanueva (II) +m. "Tinay" (?)

Notes: Mariano P. Villanueva (I) was the brother of Vicente Villanueva who, according to their granddaughter, Angela Villanueva Villanueva, moved to Bicol from Iloilo to start an Abaca and Sinamay business.[1] They formed the Mssrs. Villanueva & Company.[2] According to Ancestry.com, Mariano P. Villanueva (I) was born in 1843 and died in Manila on April 22, 1918.[3] According to court records, he was married to Teodora Arana from Legaspi in 1867.[4] They had ten children. He had several illegitimate children from different women.

According to the Philippine Supreme Court documents, from 1868 to 1910 Mariano P. (I) had liaison with a woman and produced five children four of whom were alive. He was found guilty of adultery in 1868-1900. In 1889-1890 he fathered a daughter, named Maria Villanueva, whose mother died during the American occupation. He had another affair in 1891 with another woman; in 1892-1910 he also begot children with other women.[5] According to Ancestry.com there is a Balbino B. Villanueva whose father was listed as Mariano P. Villanueva and the mother was listed as Quiteria Buenconsejo.[6] There is an existing tomb of Balbino Buenconsejo Villanueva at the Tabaco Catholic Cemetery.

Fig. 7 Picture of the tomb of Balbino Buenconsejo Villanueva- courtesy of Robert Lianco.[7]

In 1910, Teodora Arana filed for divorce but was not granted by the Philippine Supreme Court.[8] They separated after Mariano insisted that his mistress, "Lanyang"

Quijano (who used to be the girlfriend of Mariano P. Villanueva (I) before he married Teodora Arana) and their illegitimate children live with Teodora and her children under one roof at the Villanueva ancestral home at Bonifacio St., in the town of Tabaco. Teodora left and lived at their other house near the convent of the Tabaco Catholic Church. The house was later inherited by one of the legitimate daughters named, Isidora Arana Villanueva (I), who in turn sold the house to Mrs. Concepcion Peña after the WWII.[9]

All the children of Mariano P. Villanueva (I), with "Lanyang" Quijano, carried their mother's family name Quijano.

Mariano P. (I) put Teodora under very limited allowance that she had to beg from the administrator, Enrique V. Kare, for an increase in her allowance.[10] Mariano sold the ancestral home to Smith Bell and also his property in the island of San Miguel to an American, named Taylor. He bought four one-block size properties in Manila for his four illegitimate children. He lived with one of his illegitimate son[11] and died in Manila on April 22, 1918.[12]

Sources: [1, 4, 9, &11] Angela Villanueva Rios Sr. (I); [2] Lt. Charles H. Burritt; [3,6 & 12] Ancestry.com; [5 & 8] Philippine Supreme Court; ; [7] Picture of Balbino Buenconsejo Villanueva's headstone at the Tabaco Catholic Cemetery, courtesy of Robert Lianco; [10] Carlos Manuel V. Rios Sr. (I).

CHILDREN OF MARIANO P. VILLANUEVA (I) with + n.m., ufn. "LANYANG" QUIJANO

MVG-2.11	11. Felix Quijano (I) +n.m or m.(?) Maxima Bualoy[1]
MVG-2.12	12. Melania Quijano (I) +m. (?) Salcedo
MVG-2.13	13. Julio Quijano (I) +m. Rosario Abraham
MVG-2.14	14. Toribia[2] Quijano (I) +m. (?) Siquia (?)

Note: The lineage of the Quijano was given by Angela Villanueva Villanueva Rios Sr. (I) but she could not remember the name of the daughter who married Siquia.. The name "Toribia" was taken from the Facebook posting of Hector Awitin Morales Jr. (III). He did not cite his source.

Sources: Angela Villanueva Villanueva Rios Sr. (I); [1 & 2] Hector Awitin Morales's Jr. (III) Facebook posting.

CHILD OF MARIANO P. VILLANUEVA (I) with + n.m., un. (?) UNNAMED WOMAN

MVG-2.15	15. Maria Villanueva (III)

Note: The Philippine Supreme Court mentioned that the mother of Maria died during the American Occupation.

Source: Philippine Supreme Court Record Divorce Case of Teodora Arana vs. Mariano P. Villanueva in 1910;

CHILD OF MARIANO P. VILLANUEVA (I) with +n.m. QUITERIA BUENCONSEJO[1]

MVG-2.16   16. Balbino Buenconsejo Villanueva (II)[2]

Note: A tombstone **(Fig. 7)** was found and pictured by Robert Lianco. Further research in Ancestry. Com provided the name of Mariano P. Villanueva (I) as the father and Quiteria Buenconsejo as the mother.

Source: [1]Ancetry.com; [2] Robert Lianco.

SECOND GENERATION OF THE VILLANUEVA FAMILY

2ND GENERATION: VICENTE VILLANUEVA'S LINE

G2

VVG-1.1 **1. QUITERIA MABIHIS VILLANUEVA (I)**

Note: Please see the entry of Pedro Arana Villanueva Sr. (I) regarding Quiteria Mabihis Villanueva's lineage.

VVG-1.2 **2. MARIA MABIHIS VILLANUEVA (I)**

Note: She died of tuberculosis in Tabaco, Albay. She contracted the disease when she was trapped in the convent during the Filipino revolution while studying at the La Concordia Covent in Manila. The communication between Manila and the provinces were cut off during the revolution and the family could not send money to the convent for her sustenance. After the revolution her sister, Quiteria, found her in the convent emaciated and sick with tuberculosis. She was immediately taken back to Tabaco with the hope that she could recover. She later died of the disease. **End of Line.**

Source: Angela Villanueva Villanueva Rios Sr. (I)

VVG-1.3 **3. ANTONIO MABIHIS VILLANUEVA (I)**

Note: José was studying in Hong Kong when the Filipino Revolution started. He came back to the Philippines together with several Filipino students. He joined the revolutionary movement. According to Angela Villanueva Villanueva Rios Sr. (I), he was supposedly the first to deliver a revolutionary speech in English. He died in the defense of Tirad Pass with Gregorio del Pilar. He was 20 years old and single. The body was never recovered. **End of Line.**

Source: Angela Villanueva Villanueva Rios Sr. (I)

VVG-1.4 **4. BALBINO TOMAS VILLANUEVA (I)**

SON OF BALBINO TOMAS VILLANUEVA (I) with +n.m., un. **ENGLISHWOMAN**

VVG-1.4.1 1. Victor (?) Villanueva (I)

Note: Balbino Tomas Villanueva had an affair with an unnamed Englishwoman and had a son named Victor Villanueva. When Balbino's father, Vicente P. Villanueva died, Balbino and his mother moved to Spain taking with them all their inheritance, which included the pieces of furniture that were encrusted with gold and semi-precious stones. No further information regarding his life.

Source: The lineage of Balbino Villanueva is fromAngela Villanueva Villanueva Rios Sr. (I).

2ND GENERATION: MARIANO P. VILLANUEVA (I) LINE

MVG.1.1   **1. PEDRO ARANA VILLANUEVA Sr. (I)**

Fig. 8 Quiteria Mabihis Villanueva   **Fig.9** Pedro Arana Villanueva Sr.

(Both pictures courtesy of Edna Buenconsejo Lao)

CHILDREN OF PEDRO ARANA VILLANUEVA SR. (I) with his first cousin +m. QUITERIA MABIHIS VILLANUEVA[1]

VMVG-(1&2).(1&1).1	1. Vicente V. Villanueva (III) +m. Aurea Pato
VMVG-(1&2).(1&1).2	2. Felicidad V. Villanueva (I) **End of line**
VMVG-(1&2).(1&1).3	3. Leonor V. Villanueva (I) +m. José Diaz Santos
VMVG-(1&2).(1&1).4	4. Remedios V. Villanueva (I) +m. Francisco de Lejos
VMVG-(1&2).(1&1).5	5. Pedro V. Villanueva (I) +n.m. (?)
VMVG-(1&2).(1&1).6	6. Daria V. Villanueva (I) +n.m. Luis Madrid
VMVG-(1&2).(1&1).7	7. José V. Villanueva (I) +n.m. Eleuteria Bobis
VMVG-(1&2).(1&1).8	8. Angela Villanueva Villanueva (I) +m. Jesus Salvador Blance Rios Sr.

CHILD OF PEDRO ARANA VILLANUEVA (I) with +n.m. MRS. MIRASOL OF TABACO

MVG-2.1.9   9. Adriano Mirasol Sr. (I) +m. Asuncion Barbante[2]

Fig. 10 Quiteria V. Villanueva with her children and grandchildren. Front row sitting down: Celia Santos, Margarita De Lejos, Remedios de Los Angeles de Lejos; 2nd Row standing: Luz de Lejos, Elvira Villanueva, Quiteria M. Villanueva, Felicidad V. Villanueva, Muriel Villanueva de Lejos, Josefina Villanueva Santos; Back row: Jose V. Villanueva (I), Angela V. Villanueva (I), Daria V. Villanueva (I), Leonor V. Villanueva (I) and her husband Jose Diaz Santos. Family picture courtesy of Edna Buenconsejo Lao.

Fig.11 Internment of Quiteria Villanueva Villaueva. She died of Cerebral Hemorrhage on June 4, 1941 at the Doctor's Hospital in Vernmont St., Malate, Manila.

From left to right: Front Row: Muriel V. de Lejos; Josefina V. Santos; Celia V. Santos; Ruthie de Lejos (half sister of the children of Remedios Villanueva de Lejos); Erlinda V. Santos; Remedios De Los Angeles (II); Luz de Lejos; Elvira Villanueva.
Standing from left to right: Vicente P. Villanueva Jr.; Consolation (Nena) R. Calleja; Daria Villanueva and Antonio Madrid Villanueva (the head barely seen above the wreath); Salvador B. Rios; Angela V. Rios (I); Leonor V. Santos; Jose V. Villanueva (I); Rafael A. Villanueva (I); Aurea P. Villanueva; Felicidad V. Villanueva; Margarita V. de Lejos. Picture courstesy of Edna Lao of Pasay City, Philippines.

Note: Quiteria Mabihis Villanueva (I) and Pedro Arana Villanueva Sr. (I) were first cousins. Pedro was the oldest son of Mariano P. Villanueva Sr. (I). Quiteria was the oldest child and daughter of Vicente Villanueva (I). Quiteria's father, Vicente Villanueva (I) opposed the marriage at first but Quiteria and Pedro were determined to get married so, he conceded. Pedro finished Commerce in Hong Kong. He died around 1916-1917. Quiteria died on June 4, 1941 in Manila.

Muriel de Lejos Riosa (I) was the one who said that "Mabihis" was the surname of the common law wife of Vicente P. Villanueva (I) but it should be noted that the son of Pedro Arana Villanueva Sr. (I), Dr. Vicente V. Villanueva the (III), signed his middle initial "L".

According to Delia Guinto Santiago the "L" stands for Luis. Pedro's (I) and Quiteria's first son and the oldest child's full name is Vicente Luis Villanueva Villanueva (III).

Sources: [1]The lineage of Pedro and Quiteria Villanueva is from Angela Villanueva Rios Sr. (I); [2] First name of Adriano Mirasol Sr. (I) and his wife is from Mario Manalang Quijano (I) given during his visit to Santa Maria on 9/19/2018; Muriel de Lejos Riosa. Clarificar

MVG-2.2   **2. FRANCISCA ARANA VILLANUEVA (I)**

CHILDREN OF FRANCISCA ARANA VILLANUEVA (I) with +m. SANTIAGO RIOSA OF TABACO

MVG-2.2.1	1. Pilar V. Riosa (I) +m. Dr. Meliton Solano
MVG-2.2.2	2. Magin V. Riosa (I) + n. m. (?) Layug, +m. Purificacion Estevez
MVG-2.2.3	3. Consolacion V. Riosa (I) +m. Atty. Mariano Calleja No issue. **End of Line**

Fig. 12 Francisca Arana Villanueva Riosa with her son's, Magin Riosa Sr. (I), family. Picture courtesy of Corina Belle Riosa Villar of Tayhi, Tabaco, Albay.

Fig. 13 Francisca Arana Villanueva Riosa with her son's, Magin Villanueva Riosa Sr. (I), family. First row: Purita and Adela; 2nd row: Purificacion Etevez, Francisca, Magin Sr.; 3rd row: Magin Jr., Ester and Santiago (II).

Fig. 14 Magin Villanueva Riosa Sr. (I) infront of the hearse of his mother, Francisca Arana Villanueva Riosa (I) who died on May 3, 1949. The picture was taken infront of the Riosa's ancestral home. Picture courtesy of Corina Bell Riosa Villar.

Note: Francisca Arana Villanueva (I) was born in 1866. She died of heart attack on May 3, 1949 and was buried at the Tabaco Catholic Cemetery. Her husband, Santiago Riosa, was born in 1856 and died on February 16, 1922 of tuberculosis. He too was buried at the Tabaco Catholic Cemetery.

Sources: The dates of birth; dates and causes of death are from Muriel de Lejos Riosa. Pictures of Francisca with Magin V. Riosa's family are from Corina Belle Villar. Robert Lianco contributed the picture of the tombstones and Angela V. Villanueva Sr. (I) contributed the biographical and genealogical record of Francisca Arana Villanueva (I).

Fig. 15 Tombstone of Santiago Riosa and Francisca Arana Villanueva at the Tabaco Catholic Cemetery. Picture courtesy of Robert Liangco.

MVG-2.3   **3. Maria Arana Villanueva (II)**

CHILDREN OF MARIA ARANA VILLANUEVA (II) with +m. IGNACIO LIANGCO OF MALINAO

MVG-2.3.1	1. Luzon V. Liangco (I)
MVG-2.3.2	2. Amparo V. Liangco (I)
MVG-2.3.3	3. Socorro V. Liangco (I) +m. Marcial Almonte
MVG-2.3.4	4. Felicidad V. Liangco (II) +m Geronimo Ontinero

Note: Angela Villanueva Rios Sr. (I) gave the information regarding the lineage of the Liangco of Malinao.[1]

Ignacio Liangco was one of the signatories of a "document sent to the Civil Governor pledging support to Spain by prominent people from Tabaco.[2] This was during the first uprising led by Andres Bonifacio on the last days of August of 1896."[3]

To date, no further information available with regards to this family except that Luzon had moved to Manila. Repeated inquiries by Robert Liangco failed to obtain any relevant result because the data collected were confusing and do not mention Maria Villanueva as the mother.[4]

Sources: [1]Angela Villanueva Rios Sr. (I); [2] "El Comercio" published on October 1896; [3] 1953, *Lucha y Libertad*, Elias M. Ataviado, translated to English by Juan T. Ataviado, p. 6; [4]Robert Lianco.

MVG-2.4   **4. Antonio Arana Villanueva (II)**

CHILDREN OF ANTONIO ARANA VILLANUEVA (II) with +m. A SPANISH LADY NAMED TERESITA

MVG-2.4.1   1. Antonio Villanueva Jr. (III)
MVG-2.4.2   2. Pedro Villanueva (III)

Note: Antonio Arana Villanueva Sr. (II) was sent to Spain to study. He never went back to the Philippines. He stayed in Spain and married a Spanish lady named Teresita.[1] Although Angela Villanueva Rios Sr. (I) was the first source of information regarding this family, Evelyn Murillo Morales, daughter of Enrique Villanueva Morales, was the one who had actually met the sons. She had stayed with one of them and said that one of the sons owned a towel factory and the other was not well off. Eventually the towel factory went bankrupt.[2]

Sources: [1]Angela Villanueva Rios Sr. (I); [2]Evelyn Murillo Morales Bofarull (I) as told to Patricia Villanueva Rios Wood (I),

MVG-2.5   **5**. **Rafael Arana Villanueva (I)**
CHILDREN OF RAFAEL ARANA VILLANUEVA (I) with +m. MARIQUITA ZULUETA

MVG-2.5.1   1. Trinidad Z. Villanueva (I) +m. Domingo Almonte
MVG-2.5.2   2. Rafaelito Z. Villanueva (I) **No further information**
MVG-2.5.3   3. Sofia (Nena) Z. Villanueva (I) +m. Tito Crisol
MVG-2.5.4   4. Juanito Z.Villanueva (I) died single **End of Line**
MVG-2.5.5   5. Soledad Z. Villanueva (I) died single **End of Line**
MVG-2.5.6   6. Carmelo Z. Villanueva (I) +m. Filomina Salazar
MVG-2.5.7   7. Conchita Z. Villanueva (I) +m. Venancio Basco

Fig. 16 Family of Rafael Arana Villanueva and Mariquita Zulueta Front row: Soledad, Conchita and Carmelo; Seated 2nd row: Trinidad with baby Lourdes, Rafaelito, Mariquita Zulueta, Juanito and Sofia (Nena) Back row Standing: Domingo Almonte, Rafael Arana Villanueva and Tito Crisol. Picture from Marichu Crisol Reynolds's Facebook posting.

Note: Rafael Arana Villanueva maintained a mistress, Flaviana Manjares, and had children with her while married to Mariquita Zulueta. When Mariquita died due to typhus fever, Rafael married his mistress Flaviana Manjares. Juanito and Soledad died single. **End of lines**. Carmelo and his wife, Filomina Salazar, had no issue. **End of line**.

Sources: Angela Villanueva Rios Sr. (I). Vicki Zulueta Antipolo contributed the picture of Antonio Zulueta with his family at Ponape (Carolinas Island).

Fig. 17 Brother of Mariquita Zulueta while being exiled at Ponape (Carolinas Island) From left to right: Antonio Zulueta, Justina, and the nanny of Manuela, and baby Manolita. Picture courtesy of Vicki Zulueta Antipolo from Singapore.

CHILDREN OF RAFAEL ARANA VILLANUEVA (I) with +m² FLAVIANA MANJARES

MVG-2.5.8²	8. Roman M. Villanueva (I) +m. (?)
MVG-2.5.9²	9. Felipa M. Villanueva (I) +m. Ruperto Ambil
MVG-2.5.10²	10. Reynaldo M. Villanueva (I) +m. "Dodeng" (?)
MVG-2.5.11²	11. Honesto M. Villanueva (I) +m. Salvacion Morales
MVG-2.5.12²	12. Amado M. Villanueva (I) +m. Josefa Ranara +m² Andrea Encisa
MVG-2.5.13²	13. Avelina M. Villanueva (I) +m. Guillermo de la Riva
MVG-2.5.14²	14. Gloria M. Villanueva (I) +m. Atty Delfin de Vera
MVG-2.5.15²	15. Luis M. Villanueva (I) +m. Salvacion Cope

Note: Permission to include the lineage of the Rafael Arana Villanueva (I) with his 2nd wife, Flaviana Manjares, in this genealogical listing was given by Rafael Cope Villanueva of Melbourne, Australia. Antonio Morales Villanueva (VIII) on August 7. 2018 telephone conversation, gave the lineage of Honesto Manjares Villanueva. Gloria Manjares Villanueva and her husband, Atty. Delfin de Vera had no issue. **End of line.**

Sources: Angela V. Rios Sr. (I); Geni posting by Rafael Cope Villanueva; telephone comversation with Antonio Morales Villanueva (VIII) on August 7, 2018; Vicki Antipolo of Singapore.

MVG-2.6   **6. MARIANO ARANA VILLANUEVA (II)**

CHILDREN OF MARIANO ARANA VILLANUEVA (II) with +m. CONSUELO REANZARES[1] BAUTISTA Sr. OF BINONDO, MANILA

MVG-2.6.1	1. Salvador B. Villanueva (I) died single **End of Line**
MVG-2.6.2	2. Leticia B. Villanueva (I) died single **End of Line**
MVG-2.6.3	3. Mariano B. Villanueva (III) +m Rosalina Santos[2]
MVG-2.6.4	4. Raul B. Villanueva (I) **No further information**
MVG-2.6.5	5. Erlinda B. Villanueva (I) +n.m. Dr. Turla; +m Charles Glazer
MVG-2.6.6	6. Consuelo B. Villanueva (II) +m Melqueides Torres

Note: Mariano Arana Villanueva (II) studied in Spain.[3] He married a Chinese intellectual and newspaper columnist, Consuelo Reanzares Bautista from Binondo, Manila.[4] Consuelo was an accomplished pianist.[5] The family was financially ruined during the WWII. When Mariano died the family could hardly afford a decent burial for him.[6]

The children of Mariano (II) stayed at first with Leonor Villanueva Santos, the daughter of Pedro Arana Villanueva (I) and Quiteria Mabihis Villanueva (I).

Erlinda B. Villanueva (I) claimed that they were treated badly by Leonor by letting them eat soft boiled rice with "*sapal*" (shredded coconut meat residue after the milk had been squeezed out) while the family of Leonor ate regular steamed rice. She could never forgive Leonor for that.[7] In Leonor's defense, Muriel de Lejos Riosa said that they were all eating soft-boiled rice with "*sapal*"during the war and were trying very hard to make everything last longer.[8]

They also stayed with Angela V. Villanueva Rios Sr. (I). Erlinda B. Villanueva (I), however, did not complain about their stay with the family.

Sources: [1]The maiden name "Reanzares" was from Hector Awitin Morales Jr. (III) Facebook posting; [2] Elvira V. McNamara; [3&6] Angela V. Rios Sr.(I); [4&5] conversation with Consuelo Bautista Villanueva Sr. in the summer of around 1975 in San Lorenzo summer house; [7]conversation with Erlinda B. Villanueva Glazer in the summer of around 1975 in San Lorenzo summer house; [8]Muirel de Lejos Riosa; Elvira Villanueva McNamara.

Fig. 18 A plaque found at the Tabaco Municipal Building showing Mariano Arana Villanueva as one of the Councilors.

MVG-2.7   **7. Isidora Arana Villanueva (I)**

Note: Isidora Arana Villanueva was single but said to have adopted the daughter of Felix Quijano, Angela Quijano. Isidora was the only child of Teodora Arana and Mariano P. Villanueva (I) who sided with their father and his mistress "Lanyang" Quijano, who caused the split of the family of the Villanueva. Angela Bualoy Quijano, (III) daughter of Felix Quijano (I) and Maxima Bualoy was said to have been adopted by isidora Arana Villanueva. Whether she was legally adopted is unknown. **End of Line.**

Source: Common knowledge; Angela Villanueva Rios Sr. (I)

MVG-2.8   **8. Delfin Arana Villanueva Sr.(I)**

12/24/1876 – 2/21/1949

CHILDREN OF DELFIN ARANA VILLANUEVA (I) with +m. TELESFORA (PURA) ANTE OF TABACO

MVG-2.8.1	1. Fermin A. Villanueva (I) +m. Anita (?); + m^2 "Laleng"
MVG-2.8.2	2. Sigfredo A. Villanueva (I) +m. Mercedez Parcia
MVG-2.8.3	3. Dominador A. Villanueva (I) +m. Juana Lomibao
MVG-2.8.4	4. Adelaida A. Villanueva (I) +m. Juan Nicolas **End of Line**
MVG-2.8.5	5. Carlito A. Villanueva (I) **No further information**
MVG-2.8.6	6. Delfin A. Villanueva Jr. (II) +m. Herminia Chavez

Fig. 19 The tombstone of Delfin Arana Villanueva and Telesfora Ante. Picture courtesy of Robert Lianco

Note: Angela Villanueva Rios Sr. (I) gave the lineage of Delfin Arana Villanueva. She mentioned a son named Guillermo without mentioning Sigfredo's name. However, Sigfredo's name had appeared twice: from Annie Riosa Naños's and Hector Awitin Morales's Jr. (III) Facebook postings. He has been added here and Guillermo had been removed.

Delfin Arana Villanueva (I) was born on December 24, 1876 and died on February 21, 1949. Telesfora Ante was born on January 5, 1877 and died on January 11, 1926. Delfin and his wife are both buried at the Tabaco Catholic Cemetery.

Sources: Angela Villanueva Rios Sr. (I); 2018 Facebook postings of Annie Riosa Nañoz and Hector Awitin Morales Jr. (III); Robert Lianco.

MVG-2.9   **9. Candida Arana Villanueva (I)**

Fig. 20 Candida Arana Villanueva and Ramon Morales. Picture from Facebook posting "Familia Villianueva de Tabaco".

CHILDREN OF CANDIDA ARANA VILLANUEVA (I) with +m. RAMON MORALES A SPANIARD FROM TIUI.

MVG-2.9.1	1. Catalina V. Morales (I) +m. Jose de Luna Gonzales
MVG-2.9.2	2. Natalia V. Morales (I) single **End of Line**
MVG-2.9.3	3. Ramon V. Morales (I) +m. Visitacion Villanueva
MVG-2.9.4	4. Enrique V. Morales (I) +m. Trinidad Murillo
MVG-2.9.5	5. Luz V. Morales (I) +m. Benito Serrano
MVG-2.9.6	6. Lourdes (Neneng) V. Morales (I) single **End of Line**
MVG-2.9.7	7. Teodora V. Morales (II) +m Atty. Ricardo Sikat

Fig. 21 Taken during the birthday celebration of Candida Arana Villanueva Morales (I) and her niece Angela Villanueva Rios Sr. (I) at the ancestral home of the Rios family in Tabaco on Ocotber 3, 1953-1954 (?).

Front row: Maria Teresa Concepcion V. Rios; Annie Riosa Nañoz, Cynthia Morales Villanueva, Angela V, Rios Jr. (II), Yolanda Riosa Nañoz

2nd row standing: Trinidad Murillo Morales, (seated) Jose V. Rios, Carlos Manuel V. Rios, Jaime Miguel V. Rios, Virgilio Morales Villanueva, Juanito Salvador V. Rios Jr., Enrique Villanueva Morales

3rd row standing: Filomina Salazar Villanueva, (back of Filomina) Salvacion Morales Villanueva, Adela Villanueva Crisol, Gertrudes Villanueva Crisol, Maria Leticia Patricia V. Rios, Milagros (?) Villanueva, Mr. Palomo, Jesus Salvador B. Rios Sr.

4th row: Sofia Villanueva Crisol, Carmelo Villanueva Crisol, Purificacion Estevez Riosa, Candida Arana Villanueva Morales, Angela Villanueva Rios Sr., Adelaida A.Villanueva (Nicolas), Lourdes V. Morales, Nenita P. Buenaventura, Trinidad Palomo.

5th row: Magin V. Riosa Sr., (unnamed lady), Magin E. Riosa Jr., (unnamed lady), (unnamed gentleman)

Last row: Alfredo (?) Villanueva (son of Fermin Villanueva), unnamed gentleman; Gualberto V. Crisol (Beting).

Note: Ramon Morales was a Spanish *haciendero* living in Tiwi who was financially ruined due to his involvement in politics.[1] He retained land holdings in Tiwi, which were inherited by his children.[2] During their financial downturn some of the children lived with Pedro's and Quiteria's family.[3]

Angela V. Villanueva Rios Sr. (I) claimed that Catalina swindled her mother, Quiteria Mabihis Villanueva of her jewelry. This incident was well known among the children of Quiteria.[4]

Source: [1]Maria Leticia Patricia Rios Wood; [2] common knowledge; [3 & 4]Angela Villanueva Rios Sr. (I); Orestes M. Morales (I) and his wife Dolores Dy Alparce gave most of the information regarding the lineage of the Morales family on April 4, 2011 at the house of Andres V. Rios; Antonio Morales Villanueva (VIII) August 7, 2018 telephone conversation, helped identify some of the people who attended the birthday party of Candida V. Morales (I) and Angela V. Rios Sr. (I); Connie Brusuelas (I) also helped in identifying some of the attendees.

MVG-2.10 **10. Vicente Arana Villanueva (II)**

CHILDREN OF VICENTE ARANA VILLANUEVA (II) with +m. "TINAY" (?)

MVG-2.10.1   1. Rita (?) Villanueva (I) **No further information**
MVG-2.10.2   2. Antonio (?) Villanueva (IV) **No further information**

Note: Vicente Arana Villanueva (II) was sent to London to study. No further information regarding his life.

Source: Angela Villanueva Rios Sr. (I).

MVG-2.11 **11. Felix Quijano Sr. (I)**

CHILDREN OF FELIX QUIJANO Sr. (I) with +m. MAXIMA BUALOY[1]

MVG-2.11.1   1. Felix Quijano Jr. (II) +m. Mercedez Madrid
MVG-2.11.2   2. Teodoro Quijano (I) +m. Lorena Martines
MVG-2.11.3   3. Angela Quijano (II) +n.m. Montealegre

Note: According to Angela Villanueva Rios Sr. (I), Felix Quijano Sr. was about to be killed by a disgruntled tenant when Mr. Bualoy's daughter, Maxima, interfered and saved him. Felix later married Maxima.[2] No other corroborating statements available regarding this incident or circumstances.

Sources: ¹The names of the wives of Felix Quijano Sr (I), Felix Quijano Jr. (II) and Teodoro Quijano was taken from 2018 Facebook posting of Hector Awitin Morales Jr. (III); ²Angela Villanueva Rios Sr. (I);

MVG-2.12   **12. Melania Quijano (I)**

CHILDREN OF MELANIA QUIJANO (I) with +m. (?) SALCEDO

MVG-2.12.1	1. Ernistina Q. Salcedo (I) +m (?) Bautista
MVG-2.12.2	2. Enrique Q. Salcedo (II) +m. Nena Picasso

Note: No further information regarding Melania Quijano and her husband Salcedo.

Source: Angela Villanueva Rios Sr. (I); 2018 Facebook posting of Hector Awitin Morales Jr. (III).

MVG-2.13   **13. Julio Quijano (I)**

CHILD OF JULIO QUIJANO (I) with +m. ROSARIO ABRAHAM

MVG-2.13.1   1. Hector A. Quijano (I) +m. Josefina Manalang

Note: According to the telephone interview with Antonio Morales Villanueva on August 7, 2018 in California, he stated that when Julio married Rosario Abraham, she already had Hector (I). He also claimed that Hector Abaraham Quijano admitted as much during the gathering of the Villanueva relatives in San Roque, during the planned candidacy of Enrique Villanueva Morales (I).
On 2017, Rafael Cope Villanueva of Melbourne, Australia, at the request of Angela Villanueva Rios Howe Jr. (III) of California, asked his father, Luis Manjares Villanueva if he was aware of this claim, unfortunately he was not. Later Rafael emailed that his father said that if Antonio Morales Villanueva got his information from his father, Honesto (older brother of Luis) then it could be true.
After Enrique V. Kare, then Ricardo Sikat, Julio, on September 16, 1919, in behalf of the estate of Mariano P. Villanueva continued the claim against Quiteria V. Villanueva, administratrix of Pedro Arana Villanueva, for payment of loan made by Pedro A. Villanueva from his father while they were both alive. The court ruled in favor of Quiteria. The entirety of this case is in the unabridged version of the Genealogical Record of the Villanueva.

Source: Angela Villanueva Rios (I), August 7, 2018 telephone conversation with Antonio Morales Villanueva (VIII); excerpt of 2017 e-mail of Rafael Cope

Villanueva of Melbourne, Australia; Philippine Supreme Court Record, **G.R. No. L-35925   November 10, 1932, RICARDO SIKAT, Judicial Administrator of the intestate estate of the deceased Mariano P. Villanueva,** plaintiff-appellant, vs. **QUITERIA VIUDA DE VILLANUEVA, Judicial Administratrix of the intestate estate of the deceased Pedro Villanueva,** defendant-appellee.
Feria and La O for appellant. Jesus Paredes for appellee. Under "agreed statement of facts to the court: #4."

MVG-2.14.   **14. Toribia Quijano (I)**

Note: The first name, Toribia, was taken from the 2018 Facebook posting of Hector Awitin Morales Jr. (III). No other information available or other corroborating statement with regards to the name Toribia or her family except, according to Angela Villanueva Rios Sr. (I), that one of the daughters of Mariano with "Lanyang" Quijano was married to a man named Siquia. **No further information.**

Source: Angela Villanueva Rios (I) and 2018 Facebook posting of Hector Awitin Morales Jr. (III)

MVG-2.15.   **15. Maria Villanueva (III)**

Note: No further information regarding Maria Villanueva except that her mother died during the American occupation.

Source: Philippine Supreme Court Divorce Case of Teodora Arana vs. Mariano P. Villanueva of 1910. **No further information.**

MVG-2.16   **16. Balbino Buenconsejo Villanueva**
                May 7, 1896 – June 10, 1946

Fig. 22 Tombstone of Balbino Buenconsejo Villanueva. Picture courtesy of Robert Lianco of Tabaco, Albay.

Note: The name of Balbino Buenconsejo Villanueva was first noticed from Robert Liangco's pictures of tombstone at the Tabaco Catholic Cemetery. Further research at Ancestry. Com gave the father's name as Mariano P. Villanueva, and the mother's name as Quiteria Buenconsejo. Balbino Buenconsejo Villanueva is included here as one of the possible illegitimate children of Mariano P. Villanueva. **No further information.**

Source: Robert Lianco and Ancestry .com

THIRD GENERATION OF THE VILLANUEVA FAMILY

THIRD GENERATION OF THE VILLANUEVA FAMILY

G3

VVG-1.4.1   **1. Victor (?) Villanueva (I)**

Note: Victor (?) Villanueva is the son of Balbino Tomas Villanueva with an unnamed Englishwoman.

Ernestina Quijano Salcedo told Angela V. Villanueva Rios Sr. (I) that during her travels around the world she met Victor (?) Villanueva in London. According to her, Victor was one of the professors teaching at one of the Universities in London and was a very good looking gentleman like his father. **No further information**.

Source: Angela V. Villanueva Rios Sr.(I) as told by Ernestina Quijano Salcedo.

VMVG-(1&2).(1&1).1   **1. Dr. Vicente Villanueva Villanueva** (III)
                                     1894 – July 4, 1933

CHILDREN OF VICENTE VILLANUEVA VILLANUEVA (III) with + m. AUREA PATO OF PILI, CAMARINES SUR

VMVG-(1&2).(1&1).1.1	1. Vicente P. Villanueva (IV) died single **End of Line**
VMVG-(1&2).(1&1).1.2	2. Paz P. Villanueva (I) +m. (?) Casiano Guinto
VMVG-(1&2).(1&1).1.3	3. Celia P. Villanueva (I) +m. Dominador Albarico

Note: Dr. Vicente Villanueva Villanueva (III) was a Doctor of Medicine who graduated from Sto. Tomas University. One month before graduation his father, Pedro Arana Villanueva Sr. (I) died of cerebral hemorrhage. He tried to bleed him with the use of leeches but of no use.

Vicente was in love with his first cousin Pilar Villanueva Riosa but both decided to break off the relationship because they were afraid that their parents would disagree with the union.

He had another sweetheart named Layda, a nurse, but his parents told him to break off with her and to concentrate on his studies, which he did.

Years later, he met and married a teacher, Aurea Pato from Pili, Camarines Sur when he was assigned at Naga City. They later moved to Tabaco where he died of cerebral hemorrhage at the Tabaco dispensary. His mother and siblings were in Manila when he died but they immediately went back to Tabaco for his funeral. He was first buried at the Tabaco Chinese Cemetery but when Aurea moved back to Pili, she took his bones with her.

Sources: Angela Villanueva Rios Sr. (I); Edbert Villanueva Albarico, Chito Guinto; Delia Guinto Santiago.

Fig. 23 Dr. Vicente V. Villanueva seated at right with his friends. Picture courtesy of Chito Villanueva Guinto.

Fig. 24 A cropped picture of Aurea Pato Villanueva taken from the internment of Quiteria V. Villanueva in 1939. Picture courtesy of Edna Lao.

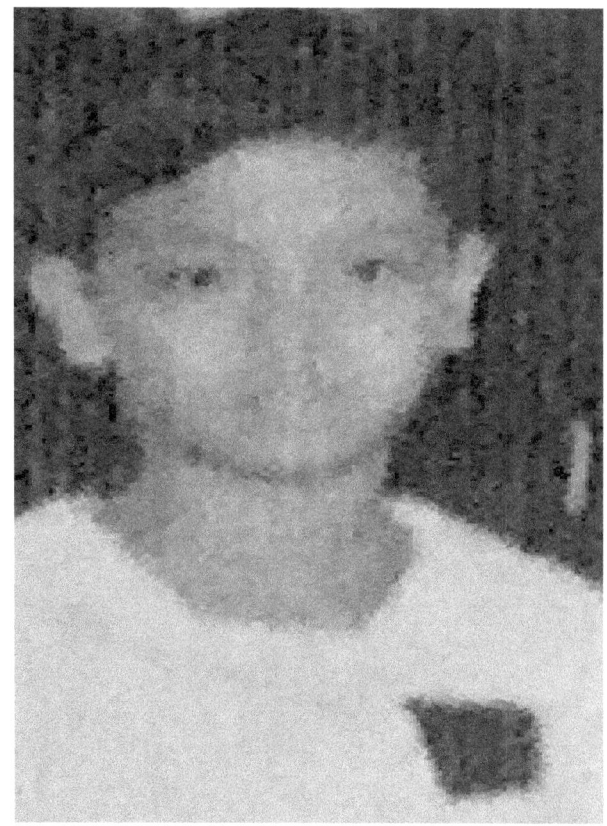

Fig. 25 Vicente Pato Villanueva Jr. (IV), son of Dr, Vicente Luis V. Villanueva and Aurea Pato. Vicente Pato Villanueva died of heart problem when he was a teenager and was originally buried at the Pili Cemetery. His remains was later transferred to Sto. Niño Cemetery in Naga City, Camarines Sur together with his father and mother.[4] Picture of Vicente Jr. (IV) was cropped and taken from a picture sent by Edna Buenconsejo Lao.

Fig. 26 Paz Pato Villanueva's university graduation picture. Picture courtesy of the Guinto family.

Fig. 27 Celia Pato Villanueva's university graduation picture. Picture courtesy of the Albarico Family.

VMVG-(1&2).(1&1).2   **2. Felicida Villanueva Villanueva (I)**
March 7, (?) – May 19, 1969

Fig. 28 Felicidad Villanueva Villanueva (I) high school graduation picture. Picture courtesy of Edna Buenconsejo Lao of Pasay City, Philippines.

Fig. 29 Felicidad, far right carrying her niece, Margarita while her sister Remedios is carrying baby Muriel. Picture courtesy of Corina Belle Villar

Fig. 30 Felicidad with Antonio Villanueva (Madrid). Picture from of Edna Buenconsejo Lao

Note: Felicidad Villanueva Villanueva had a lot of suitors but was in love with her boyfriend, Lt. Jose Dizon. They were expected to marry but when Lt. Dizon met Mirasol's daughter, he had an affair with her. Lt. Dizon ended up marrying her.

Afterwards, Felicidad did not entertain any more suitors and lived a single life. She spent her lifetime taking care and raising the children of her sister, Remedios Villanueva de Lejos, who died from childbirth. She also helped raised the daughter of her brother Pedro V. Villanueva jr. (II) who died when he contracted tuberculosis; and the son of her other sister, Daria V.Villanueva, with their cousin Luis Madrid.

Felicidad died of Cardiac Arrest.

Source: Common knowledge among the Villanueva family; Angela V. Rios Sr. (I) dates and cause of death was given by Edna Lao through telephone conversation on 3/23/2019 at 7:15 P.M., California time.

VMVG-(1&2).(1&1). 3   **3. Leonor Villanueva Villanueva (I)**
                                      9/27/1896 – 8/6/1973

CHILDREN OF LEONOR VILLANUEVA VILLANUEVA (I) with +m. JOSE DIAZ SANTOS OF MARIQUINA, RIZAL

VMVG-(1&2).(1&1).3.1   1. Josefina Villanueva Santos (I) +m. Dorito Tuaño
VMVG-(1&2).(1&1).3.2   2. Celia Villanueva Santos (II) died single **End of Line**
VMVG-(1&2).(1&1).3.3   3. Erlinda Nieves Villanueva Santos (II) +m. Rolando Duria

Fig. 31 Leonor Villanueva Villanueva (I). Picture courtesy of Edna Buenconsejo Lao

Fig. 32 Leonor shown with her three daughters: Cecilia, Erlinda and Josefina. Picture from Facebook posting of Jose Tuaño of Miami, Florida.

Note: According to Angela Villanueva Rios Sr. (I), Leonor was in love with Dr. Clemenia from Tiwi who became a victim of shotgun marriage. Dr. Clemenia's parents helped him escaped to Japan on the evening of his wedding. He came back ten years later and wanted to marry Leonor but Leonor was afraid that should she marry him she had to go to Japan. She was afraid to live in Japan because she did not speak the language and she wanted to stay in the Philippines to be near her family. Despite the encouragement of her parents to marry Dr. Clemenia, if she really loved him, she refused. Many years later she married Atty. Jose Diaz Santos from Marikina, Rizal.

Margarita de Lejos Buenconsejo and her husband, Anastacio Buenconsejo, claimed that Jose Santos land grabbed Margarita's inherited properties and even the land properties that Anastacio Buenconsejo inherited from his father, Anatolio Buenconsejo. Jose Santos was able to put the properties' titles in his name and to his wife's, Leonor's, name.

Leonor died of Cancer of the lungs. She was buried with her husband at the Loyola Cemetery in Manila.

Fig. 33 Erlinda Nieves Santos, youngest daughter of Leonor Villanueva and José Diaz Santos

Sources: Angela Villanueva Rios Sr. (I); Erlinda Nieves Santos Duria; Carlos Manuel V. Rios; Jose S. Tuaño Facebook posting; telephone conversation with Edna Buenconsejo Lao on 3/23/2019 at 7:15 P.M. California time.

VMVG-(1&2).(1&1).4   4. Remedios Villanueva Villanueva (I)

CHILDREN OF REMEDIOS VILLANUEVA VILLANUEVA (I) with +m.
FRANCISCO DE LEJOS Sr. OF ALBAY

VMVG-(1&2).(1&1).4.1	1. Margarita V. de Lejos (I) +m Anastacio Burce Buenconsejo
VMVG-(1&2).(1&1).4.2	2. Francisco V. de Lejos Jr.– died when he was five. **End of Line**
VMVG-(1&2).(1&1).4.3	3. Muriel V. de Lejos (I) +m Santiago E. Riosa
VMVG-(1&2).(1&1).4.4	4. Luz Villanueva de Lejos (II) single **End of Line**
VMVG-(1&2).(1&1).4.5	5. Sofia Remedios de los Angeles Villanueva de Lejos (I) +m Rolando Pleta

Note: Remedios Villanueva Villanueva (I) was studying at Centro Escolar de Señoritas as an "interna" when she met Francisco de Lejos, a second year pre-med student from Santo Tomas University. They got married in Camarines Sur against the will of the parents of Remedios because they were still very young. Her older brother, Dr. Vicente Villanueva (II), witnessed their marriage. Dr. Vicente Villanueva (III) signed his name with a middle initial of "L", which stood for Luis.

Remedios died from complication after giving birth to her youngest daughter, Sofia Remedios de los Angeles. Quiteria Villanueva's family raised the children. When Quiteria died, Felicidad took over caring for all of them till they were grown up. Francisco de Lejos remarried but was very close to his children.

Sources: Angela Villanueva Rios Sr.(I); Muriel de Lejos Riosa (I); Margarita de Lejos Buenconsejo; Corina Belle Riosa Villar; Edna Lao's telephone call on 3/23/2019 at 7:15 P. M. California time; Grace Pleta Herrera.

Fig. 34 Enlarged and cropped picture of Remedios V. Villanueva while studying at the Centro Escolar de Señoritas as an "*interna*".

Fig. 35 Remedios and her youngest sister, Angela. Picture courtesy of Corina Bell Villar.

Fig. 36 The "Internas" of Centro Escolar de Señoritas. Remedios is the last person on the 2nd row on the far right. Picture courtesy of Edna Buenconsejo Lao.

Fig. 37 Francisco de Lejos – L-R fourth standing at the back. Picture courtesy of Edna Lao

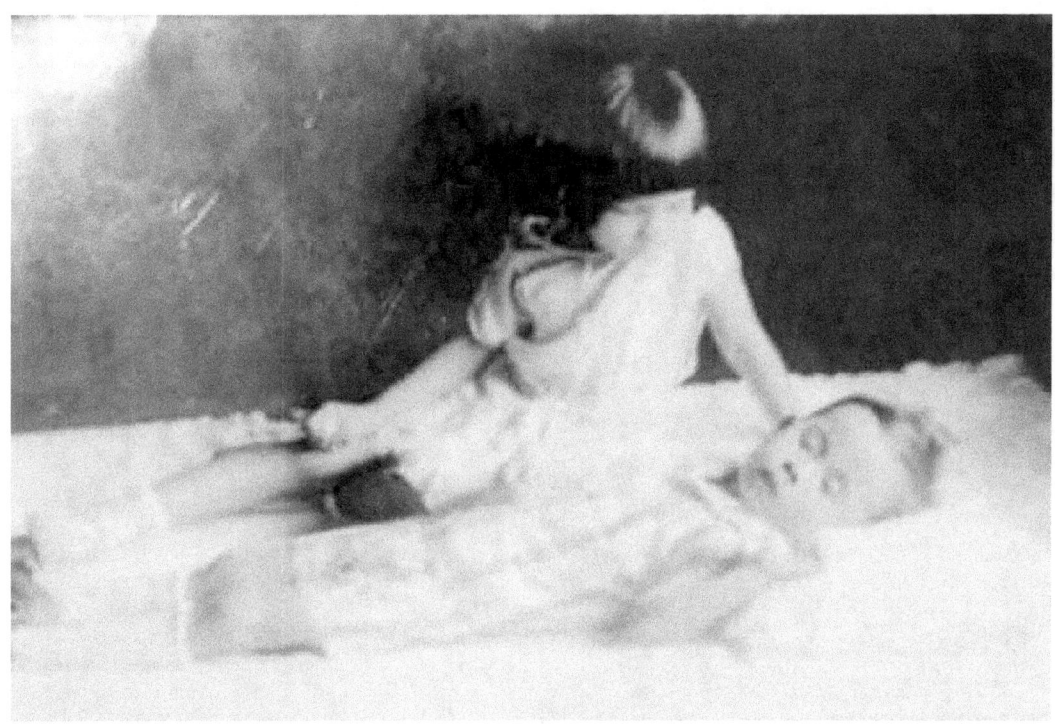

Fig. 38 Margarita looking down at her younger brother Francisco Jr. while he is sleeping. ,Francisco Jr. was the second child of Remedios V. Villanueva and Francisco de Lejos Sr. He was born in 1926 and died in 1931 at the age of five. Picture courtesy of Edna lao.

Fig. 39 Front: Antonio (Pocholo) Villanueva. From L-R: Luz de Lejos, Muriel Riosa and Sofia Remedios de los Angeles. Picture courtesy of Edna B. Lao

Fig. 40 The first grandchildren. Front: Erlinda Nieves Santos. Second row seated from L-R: Josefina V. Santos, Sofia Remedios de Los Angeles de Lejos, Celia V. Santos. 3rd row from L-R: Antonio Villanueva (Madrid), Elvira Villanueva, Margarita de Lejos, Muriel de Lejos and Luz de Lejos

VMVG-(1&2).(1&1).5   **5. Daria Villanueva Villanueva (I)**
                        10/19/1912 – 1/9/1982

CHILD OF DARIA VILLANUEVA VILLANUEVA (I) with + n.m. LUIS MADRID
OF MALINAO

VMVG-(1&2).(1&1).5.1   1. Antonio (Pocholo) Villanueva (IV) +m Elsa
                                   Buenaventura

Fig. 41 Daria Villanueva Villanueva. Picture courtesy of Edna Buenconsejo Lao

Note: Daria was born in October 1912. She studied at Centro Escolar de Señoritas. She had an affair with her couisin, Luis Madrid of Malinao and had a son with him named Antonio (Pocholo) Villanueva (III)

According to Maria Leticia Patricia R. Wood, whenever Antonio was in Tabaco, he would visit his father, Luis Madrid in Malinao.

Daria helped her son, Antonio and his wife establish a business. She lived with them for a while but for some reason things did not work out. She went back to live in Pasay again.

Daria died on January 9, 1982 of Cardiac Arrest.

Source: Angela Villanueva Rios (I); Maria Leticia Patricia R. Wood; Amelia Madrid Lopez; birth date and date of death was researched by Edna Buenconsejo Lao and the information was transmitted through telephone call on 3/23/2019 at 7:15 P.M., California time.

VMVG-(1&2).(1&1). 6   **6. Pedro Villanueva Villanueva Jr. (II)**
                            DOD: July 28, 1937

CHILD OF PEDRO VILLANUEVA VILLANUEVA (II) with +n.m. AN UNNAMED WOMAN FROM LEGASPI

VMVG-(1&2).(1&1).6.1   1. Elvira Villanueva (I)

Note: As a cadet, during a rained out parade from their school, Lyceum de Manila, Pedro was hospitalized with pneumonia but his conditioned worsened to tuberculosis. He was sent back home to Tabaco to recuperate and was treated by his brother Dr. Vicente V.Villanueva Sr. (II). Pedro's life was prolonged because of the meticulous medical care of Vicente.

Bored with provincial life, every now and then Pedro would go to Legaspi with friends to gallivant. One time, his car broke down. Instead of having it fix by a mechanic, he left it at the side of the road to rot.

He made an unnamed woman pregnant and the child was named Elvira. When the daughter was two years old, the mother of Elvira went to see the Villanueva family and gave up her daughter to Quiteria with the hope that she would be educated and given a chance to marry properly. Elvira finished university and married an Ophthalmologist, Dr. Rey Garcia.

Source: Angela Villanueva Rios Sr. (I); Conversation with Carlos Manuel Villanueva Rios Sr. (I) at his house in La Verne on March 19, 2019.

Fig. 42 Elvira Villanueva with her husband Dr. Rey Garcia and their two children. (Right) Maria Rae Cynthia Garcia and (left) Peter Raymond Garcia.

VMVG- (1&2).(1&1). 7   **7. José Villanueva Villanueva Sr. (II)**
                                   October 23, 1907 – June 15, 1976

CHILDREN OF JOSE VILLANUEVA VILLANUEVA Sr. (II) with n.m.
ELEUTERIA BOBIS OF PANAL

VMVG-(1&2).(1&1).7.1	1. Conchita B. Villanueva (II) +m Carlos Jaymalin
VMVG-(1&2).(1&1).7.2	2. Eduardo B. Villanueva (I) +m Editha Sulo
VMVG-(1&2).(1&1).7.3	3. Jose B. Villanueva Jr. (III) +m Evelyn Gregorio

VMVG-(1&2).(1&1).7.4   4. Pedro B. Villanueva (IV) +m Iluminada Bazar
VMVG-(1&2).(1&1).7.5   5. Teresa B. Villanueva (I) +m Porferio Patiag
VMVG-(1&2).(1&1).7.6   6. Gloria Natividad B. Villanueva (I) Edison Pingol
VMVG-(1&2).(1&1).7.7   7. Fe Nancy B. Villanueva (I) +m Amor Gumabao
VMVG-(1&2).(1&1).7.8   8. Rosemarie Joy B. Villanueva (I) +m Zoilo Moran

Fig. 43 The tombstone of José V. Villanueva Sr. (II). Picture taken in 2017 at the Tabaco Catholic Cemetery.

Note: After graduation as Industrial Engineer Jose Villanueva Villanueva (II) ran away with the 16 year old stepdaughter of a renter at the Villanueva house. The Step-father sued Jose and he was imprisoned for a year. After getting out from prison, frustrated that he could no longer qualify to take the board examination for licensing, he was sent to the province by Quiteria with money to build a house. With money and a car, he went to enjoy himself instead.

José had an affair and eventually lived with Eleuteria Bobis, the daughter of one of the tenants and had several children with her. He supported the family by going into "bakya" making business and other businesses. With all his businesses, he would be very successful at first but then he would end up bankrupted. His sister, Angela V. Rios Sr. (I) blamed Eleuteria for mishandling the money.

Quiteria never accepted Eleuteria. She refused Eleuteria from setting foot in Pasay. When Quiteria died, her children did not mind Eleuteria visiting but Eleuteria never did.

Despite living with Eleuteria for a long time and having eight children with her, Jose refused to marry her because he believed that "landlords never marry their tenants or their tenants' children."

Jose died of ulcerative colitis at the Andres -Maria Rios Memorial Hospital in San Isidro, Malilipot, Albay on June 15, 1976. Mrs. Abada and Mrs. Peña who owned the hospital wrote off most of his medical bills.

Sources: Angela Villanueva Rios Sr. (I), common knowledge; the lineage of José was taken from his family tree done by Robert Lianco; Margarita de Lejos Buenconsejo; Edna Buenconsejo Lao telephone conversation with Angela V. Rios Howe Jr. (III) on 3/23/2019 at 7:15 P. M. and on April 27, 2019 at 5:46 P.M. California time.

VMVG-(1&2).(1&1). 8   **8. Angela Villanueva Villanueva Sr. (I)**
October 3, 1910 – March 29, 1992

CHILDREN OF ANGELA VILLANUEVA VILLANUEVA (I) with +m JESUS SALVADOR BLANCE RIOS.

VMVG-(1&2).(1&1).8.1	1. Maria Leticia Patricia V.Rios (I) +m Charles Wood
VMVG-(1&2).(1&1).8.2	2. José V. Rios (IV) single
VMVG-(1&2).(1&1).8.3	3. Juanito Salvador V. Rios (I) +m Ester Fenix
VMVG-(1&2).(1&1).8.4	4. Emma Victoria V. Rios Palomar (I) +m Ricardo Diño.
VMVG-(1&2).(1&1).8.5	5. Carlos Manuel V. Rios (I) +m Emma Peralta
VMVG-(1&2).(1&1).8.6	6. Maria Teresa Concepcion V. Rios (I) +m Dr. Resurrecion B. Kare
VMVG-(1&2).(1&1).8.7	7. Jaime Miguel V. Rios (I) +m Amelia Fragante
VMVG-(1&2).(1&1).8.8	8. Angela V. Rios Jr. (III) +m Tony Ming Yee Howe
VMVG-(1&2).(1&1).8.9	9. Andres V. Rios (I) +m Corazon P. Molina
VMVG-(1&2).(1&1).8.10	10. Cesar Antonio V. Rios (I) single

Note: Angela Villanueva Villanueva (I) was born on October 3, 1910, the youngest and the 8th child of Pedro Arana Villanueva Sr (I) and Quiteria Mabihis Villanueva (I). Angela's father, Pedro, died when she was about 6-7 years old while she was going to Alhambra primary school. She lived a luxurious life while growing up. She drove her own car and only buys and uses silk underwear according to Margarita de Lejos Buenconsejo.

She was the only daughter who was told to finish a profession instead of finishing school not only because their family finances were dwindling but because Quiteria wanted to revived their Pharmacy store they used to own in Tabaco. Angela was supposed to work with her brother, Dr. Vicente V. Villanueva Sr. (II), unfortunately, Vicente died three years before Angela graduated from Pharmacy school.

Angela finished Pharmacy at Centro Escolar de Señoritas in 1936. While in Tabaco, a month before she was to marry Carlos Bernabe, her cousin Letty Bautista villanueva and their friend, Luisa Manalang Cabiles, introduced her to Salvador Blance Rios, the only son of the mestizo Chinese, Andres Ty Rios. Salvador just came back from a ten-year stay in the United States. They had a whirlwind courtship and within a week they were married in Tiwi in a Civil Ceremony on May 25, 1939. After a month they were married at the Tabaco Catholic church on June 25, 1939. Quiteria disowned her.

In the late 1970's, Carlos Manuel Villanueva Rios Sr.(I), her son, sponsored her to immigrate to the States after her husband, Salvador, died.

Angela lived in Monrovia, California with her son, Andres Villanueva Rios, (I) and his family for quite a while before she went home to the Philippines. She died at the Estevez Memorial Hospital on March 29, 1992 of multiple organ failure associated with old age.

Sources: Angela Villanueva Rios Sr. (I); Margarita de Lejos Buenconsejo (I); Flora Blance Rios Palomar; Carlos Manuel V. Rios Sr. (I); Jaime Miguel Rios and his wife, Amelia Fragante Rios.

Fig. 44 The graduation picture of Angela V. Villanueva from College of Pharmacy, Centro Escolar de Señoritas. Picture courtesy of Jaime Miguel Rios and Amelia Fragante Rios

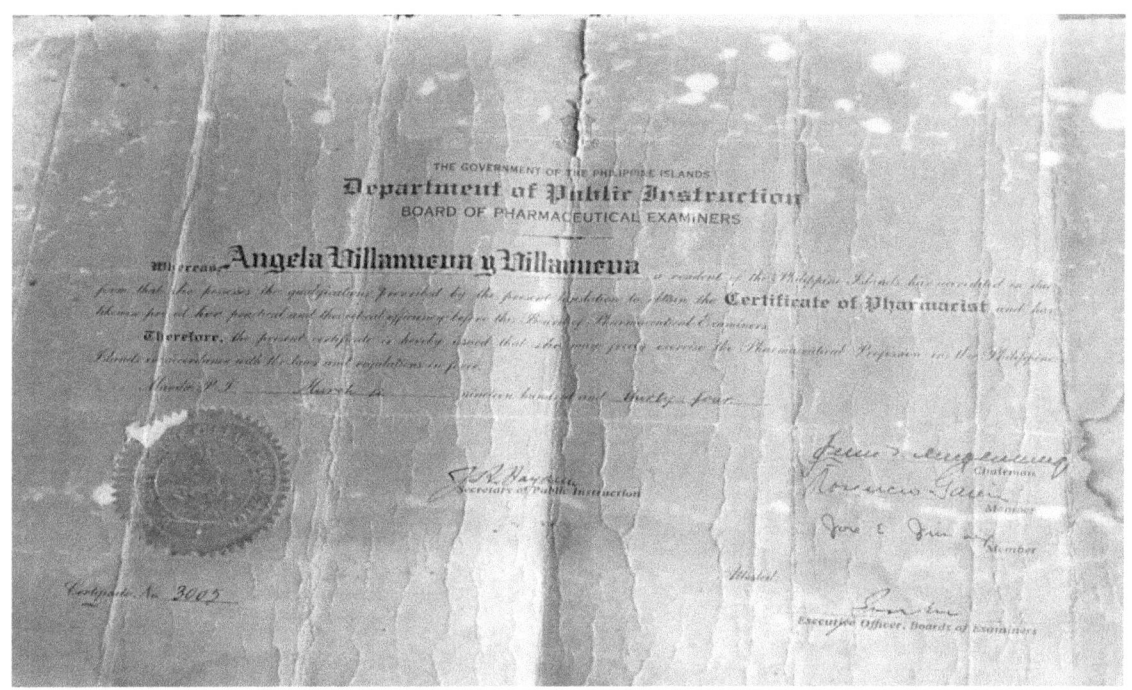

Fig. 45 Angela"s Certification. Courtesy of Jaime Miguel V. Rios and Amelia Fragante Rios

Fig. 46 Angela at the Luneta. Picture was taken by Mr. Phatana Lampoon in 1936.

Fig. 47 Angela V. Villanueva at the upstairs foyer of the Rios ancestral home after her Church wedding to Jesus Salvador Blance Sr. on June 25, 1939.

Fig. 48 Angela V. Villanueva and Salvador B. Rios with their sponsors, Mr. and Mrs. Manalang in front steps of the Rios house.

Fig. 49 The Children of Angela V. Villanueva and Salvador B. Rios in front of the Rios ancestral house in Tabaco. Front row from L-R: Andres Rios and Cesar Antonio; 2nd row from L-R, Maria Leticia Patricia, José, Juanito Salvador, Emma Victoria, Carlos Manuel, Maria Teresa Concepcion, Jaime Miguel, and Angela.

Fig. 50 Angela V. Villanueva and Salvador B. Rios with their children. Picture courtesy of Antonio V. Rios

VMVG-2.1.9   **9. Adriano Mirasol Sr. (I)**

CHILDREN OF ADRIANO MIRASOL with +m. ASUNCION BARBANTE

MVG-2.1.9.1	1. Manuel B. Mirasol (I) +m Hilda Macabeo
MVG-2.1.9.2	2. Fe B. Mirasol (I) +m Vicente de la Cruz
MVG-2.1.9.3	3. Ramon B. Mirasol (II) +m Ruby Manalang
MVG-2.1.9.4	4. Adriano B. Mirasol Jr. (II) +m Araceli Bañez
MVG-2.1.9.5	5. Willie May B. Mirasol single **End of Line**
MVG-2.1.9.6	6. Arniel B. Mirasol +m Sandra Escudero
MVG-2.1.9.7	7. Neime Mirasol (adopted)

Note: Adriano Mirasol was the son of Pedro Arana Villanueva (I) with their neighbor Mrs. Mirasol. According to the story, Pedro would take several shoes to Mr. Mirasol, who owned a shoe repair shop across the street, to keep him busy while Pedro had an affair with Mr. Mirasol's wife.

Adriano's Mirasol siblings accepted the fact that he was the son of Pedro Arana Villanueva. According to Angela V. Rios Sr. (I), Adriano's Mirasol siblings used to taunt him that he was a Villanueva and did not deserve to inherit from their father,

Adriano was very close to his half sister Angela Villanueva Rios Sr. (I). The lineage of Adriano Mirasol's family was given by Mario Manalang Quijano (I) on July 20, 2018 during a telephone conversation with Angela Villanueva Rios Howe Jr. (III), and during Mario's visit with his wife on 9/19/2018 to Santa Maria, California.

Source: Angela Villanueva Rios Sr. (I), Carlos Manuel V. Rios Sr. (I), Tiong Nanoy Borjal; July 23, 2018 at 2:27 P.M. California time, text from Mario Manalang Quijano (I).

MVG-2.2.1.   **10. Pilar Villanueva Riosa (I)**
                    1896 – July 7, 1920

CHILD OF PILAR VILLANUEVA RIOSA (I) with +m. DR. MELITON SOLANO

MVG-2.2.1.1   1. Hector R. Solano (II)

Note: Pilar Riosa Solano died from childbirth and the baby died seven months and 8 days later. They were both buried at the Solano's Mausoleum at the Tabaco Catholic Cemetery. Dr. Meliton Solano never remarried but had several mistresses and fathered a daughter, Sonia Solano, who built a mauseleum and transferred the remains of Pilar and Hector into the newly built structure.

Sources: Muriel de Lejos Riosa (I); Corina Belle Riosa Villar; Robert Lianco

Fig. 51 Pilar Riosa Solano's tombstone. Picture courtesy of Robert Lianco.

Fig. 52 Hector Riosa Solano's tombstone at the Tabaco Catholic Cemeetery. Picture courtesy of Robert Lianco.

MVG-2.2.2   11. Consolacion Villanueva Riosa (I)

CONSOLACION VILLANUEVA RIOSA AND HER HUSBAND ATTY. MARIANO CALLEJA HAD NO ISSUE. END OF LINE.

Fig. 53 Post card from Consolacion sent to Pedro and Quiteria Villanueva. Courtesy of Corina Belle Riosa Villar.

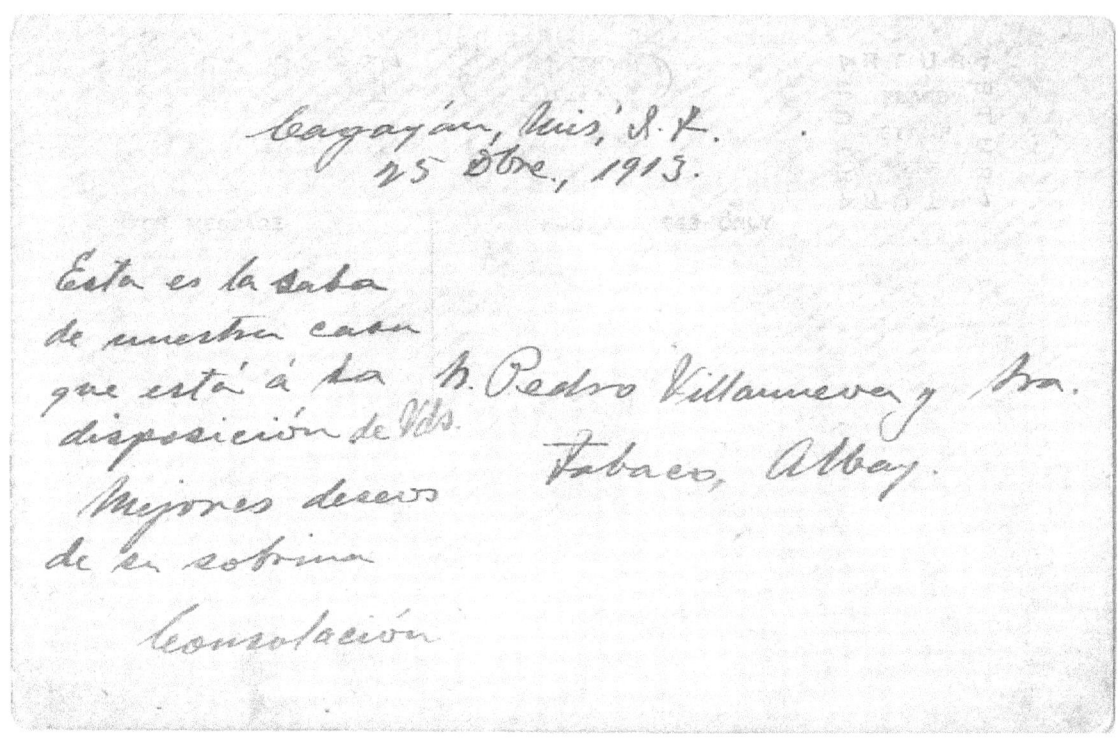

Fig. 54. The back of the postcard sent to Pedro and Quiteria Villanueva. Picture courtesy of Corina Belle Riosa Villar.

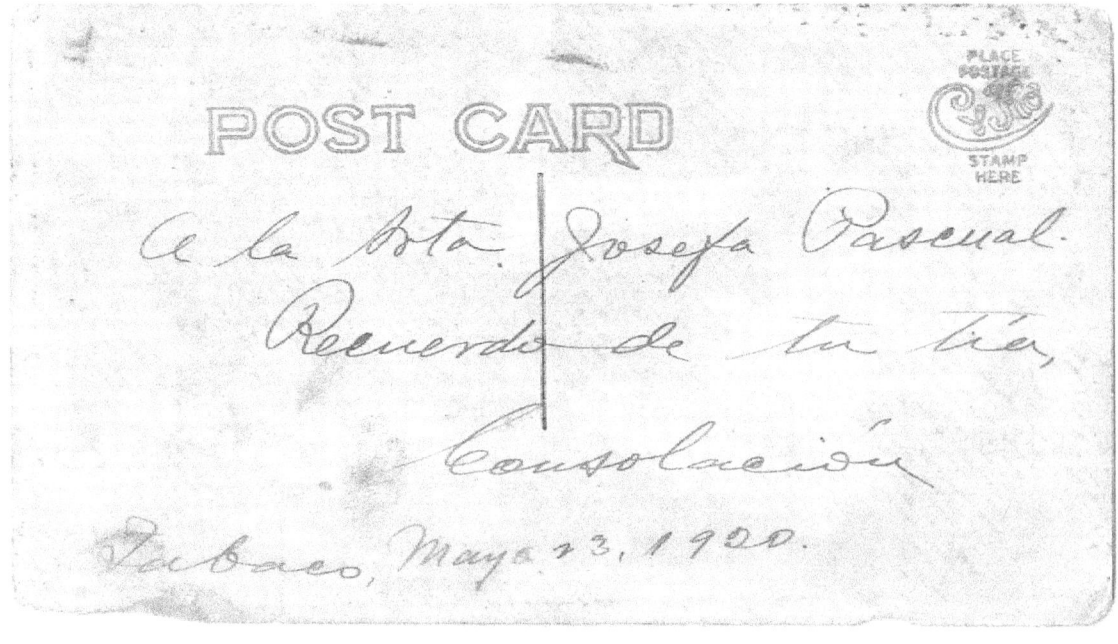

Fig. 55 The back of the picture on the following page

Fig. 56 Consolacion Riosa Calleja and Mariano Calleja. Picture courtesy of Corina Belle Villar

Note: Consolacion Villanueva Riosa (I) and her husband Atty. Mariano Calleja has no known issue but "adopted a boy who also became a lawyer. They traveled a lot because Mariano Calleja was a judge and was assigned to different places. When Mariano died, their adopted son convinced Consolacion to sell all her properties and both of them moved to Manila. He financially ruined and later abandoned her. Consolacion acquired debts playing *entre cuatro*.

"After the WWII she stayed at Pasay with the Villanueva family. She opposed the marriage of her nephew, Santiago Estevez Riosa to his first cousin, Muriel Villanueva de Lejos, saying that Muriel was a playgirl and has three other siblings who will share the inheritance from their mother, Consolacion's cousin, Remedios V. Villanueva. She suggested that Santiago marry Elvira, who was the only daughter and the sole heir of, Pedro V. Villanueva Jr. who was the younger brother of Remedios.

"When the daughters of Magin V. Riosa Sr. (I) and Purificacion Estevez, Pilar, Ester and Adela, went to study in Manila, Consolacion lived with them at Balic-Balic, Sampaloc, Manila. She went home to Tabaco briefly to attend her mother's funeral. She died of dysentery. Her brother, Magin Sr. did not know her financial situation and that she had died destitute.

"The relatives from Pasay contributed to help with the funeral dress. She was buried in one of the public cemetery in Manila." [2]

Source: [1]Angela V. Rios Sr. (I) ; [2]Muriel de Lejos Riosa (I) through Corina Belle Riosa Villar e-mail and telephone interview on October 12, 2015. Pictures were contributed by Corina Belle Riosa Villar.

MVG-2.2.3   **12. Magin Villanueva Riosa (I)**
                 8/19, 1893 – 3/1/1969

CHILDREN OF MAGIN VILLANUEVA RIOSA Sr. (I) with +nm. (?) LAYOG

MVG-2.2.3.1	1. Mario Layog (I)
MVG-2.2.3.2	2. Emma Layog (I)
MVG-2.2.3.3	3. (?) Layog

CHILDREN OF MAGIN VILLANUEVA RIOSA Sr. (I) with +m. PURIFICACION ESTEVEZ OF LEGASPI (3/22/1892 – 6/18/1978)

MVG-2.2.3.4	4. Pilar E. Riosa (II) +m Santiago Castro
MVG-2.2.3.5	5. Ester E. Riosa (I) +m Dr. Onisimo Bruselas Sr.
MVG-2.2.3.6	6. Adela E. Riosa (I) +m Col. Hermenegildo Nañoz Sr.
MVG-2.2.3.7	7. Santiago E. Riosa (II) +m Muriel V. de lejos
MVG-2.2.3.8	8. Josefina E. Riosa (II) +m Job Ala
MVG-2.2.3.9	9. Magin E. Riosa Jr. (II) +m Iluminada Layog +m^2 Elba Jesalva
MVG-2.2.3.10	10. Purita E. Riosa (I) +m Marcelo Peña

Note: Magin Villanueva Riosa Sr. (I) was born on August 19, 1893. He was a dentist. He had a common-law wife named Layog and they were living in Manila before he married Purificacion Estevez. Magin and Layog had three children. One was a soldier who died during the WWII. No further information regarding this line.

Magin also had seven children with his wife, Purificacion Estevez, and lived in the Riosa's ancestral home in Tabaco where he practiced dentistry. He died of Prostitis on March 1, 1969 and was buried at the Tabaco Catholic Cemetery. His wife, Purificacion Estevez who was born on March 22, 1892 died on June 18, 1978.

Source: Muriel de Lejos Riosa; Corina Belle Riosa Villar; Facebook posting of Hector Awitin Morales Jr (III); Robert Lianco.

Fig. 57 Clockwise: Josefina, Santiago, Purificacion, Magin Sr., Pilar, Ester, and Adela. Picture courtesy of Corina Belle Riosa Villar,

Fig. 58 Tombstone of Magin Villanueva Riiosa Sr. (I), and his wife Purificacion Estevez at the Tabaco Catholic Cemetery. Picture courtesy of Robert Lianco.

Fig. 59 Front: Santiago; L-R Ester, Pilar, Purita and Magin Jr. Matagbac 1991. Picture from Toti Quijano Facebook posting 7/7/2013.

MVG-2.3.1 **13. Luzon Villanueva Liangco (I)**

Note: To date, no further information regarding Luzon Villanueva Liangco's family except that he had a daughter and had moved to Manila.

CHILD OF LUZON VILLANUEVA LIANGCO with +m. (?)

MVG-2.3.1.1 1. Francisca (?) Liangco (II)

Sources: Angela Villanueva Rios Sr. (I). Robert Lianco gave the name of Luzon's daughter, Francisca.

MVG-2.3.2 **14. Amparo Villanueva Liangco (I)**

Note: To date, no further information regarding Amparo Villanueva Liangco's family.

Sources: Angela Villanueva Rios Sr. (I); Robert Lianco

MVG-2.3.3 **15. Socorro Villanueva Liangco (I)**

CHILDREN OF SOCORRO VILLANUEVA LIANGCO with +m MARCIAL ALMONTE SR.

MVG-2.3.3.1	1. Edgar V. Almonte (I)
MVG-2.3.3.2	2. Eleanor V. Almonte (I)
MVG-2.3.3.3	3. Marcial V. Almonte Jr. (I)

Note: Socorro Villanueva Liangco married Marcial Almonte. To date, no further information regarding Socorro Villanueva Liangco's family besides her having three children with her husband, Marcial Almonte Sr.

Sources: Angela Villanueva Rios (I); Robert A. Lianco

MVG-2.3.4 **16. Felicidad Villanueva Liangco (II)**

CHILDREN OF FELICIDAD VILLANUEVA LIANGCO with +m GERONIMO ORTINERO SR.

MVG-2.3.4.1	1. Antonio L. Ortinero (V)
MVG-2.3.4.2	2. Teresita L. Ortinero (I)
MVG-2.3.4.3	3. Geronimo L. Ortinero Jr. (I)
MVG-2.3.4.4	4. Danilo L. Ortinero (I)

MVG-2.3.4.5	5. Malou L. Ortinero (I)
MVG-2.3.4.6	6. Eric L. Ortinero (I)
MVG-2.3.4.7	7. Meyin L. Ortinero (I)

Note: The lineage of Felicidad Villanueva Liangco was given by Robert Lianco.

Sources: Angela Villanueva Rios Sr. (I); Robert Lianco.

MVG-2.4.1   **17. Antonio (?) Villanueva Jr. ((II) (Spain)**

Note: To date, no further available information regarding Antonio (?) Villanueva (II) except that he lives in Spain.

Sources: Angela Villanueva Rios Sr. (I), and Evelina Morales Bofarull (I) through Patricia Rios Wood (I)

MVG-2.4.2   **18. Pedro (?) Villanueva (III) (Spain)**

Note: To date, no further available information regarding Pedro (?) Villanueva (III) except that he lives in Spain.

Sources: Angela Villanueva Rios Sr. (I), and Evelina Morales Bofarull (I) through Patricia Rios Wood (I).

MVG-2.5.1   **19. Trinidad Zulueta Villanueva (I)**

CHILDREN OF TRINIDAD ZULUETA VILLANUEVA (I) with +m. DOMINGO ALMONTE

MVG-2.5.1.1	1. Lourdes V. Almonte (I) +n.m. "Abing" Rocha
MVG-2.5.1.2	2. Mariano V. Almonte (IV) **No further information**
MVG-2.5.1.3	3. Antonio V. Almonte (VI) +m Pilar de Castro
MVG-2.5.1.4	4. Maria V. Almonte (IV) single **End of Line**
MVG-2.5.1.5	5. Teresita V. Almonte (II) +m Dr. "Mino" Valenzuela
MVG-2.5.1.6	6. Soledad V. Almonte (II) single **End of Line**

Note: The lineage of Trinidad V. Almonte (I) was given by Angela V. Rios Sr. (I) and the names of their spouses were taken from the Facebook posting of Hector Awitin Morales Jr. (III).

Sources: Angela Villanueva Rios Sr. (I); Hector Awitin Morales Jr. (III)

MVG-2.5.2   20. Rafaelito Zulueta Villanueva

NO FURTHER INFORMATION REGARDING RAFAELITO ZULUETA VILLANUEVA LINE

MVG-2.5.3   **21. Sofia (Nena) Zulueta Villanueva (I)**

CHILDREN OF SOFIA (NENA) ZULUETA VILLANUEVA (I) with +m.TITO CRISOL

MVG-2.5.3.1   1. Juanito V. Crisol (II)
MVG-2.5.3.2   2. Amalia V. Crisol (I) +m (?) Alpasan
MVG-2.5.3.3   3. Rodolfo V. Crisol (I)
MVG-2.5.3.4   4. Adela V. Crisol (II) +m Dr. (?) Adornado
MVG_2.5.3.5   5. Marichu V. Crisol (I) +m (?) Reynolds
MVG-2.5.3.6   6. Gregorio V. Crisol (I)
MVG-2.5.3.7   7. Clemente V. Crisol (I)
MVG-2.5.3.8   8. Gualberto V. Crisol (I)
MVG-2.5.3.9   9. Soledad V. Crisol (III) +m (?) Earle Spangler
MVG-2.5.3.10   10. Asuncion V. Crisol (I) +m (?) George Cooper
MVG-2.5.3.11   11. Gertrudez V. Crisol (I) +m (?) Toto Bautista
MVG-2.5.3.12   12. Alice V. Crisol (I) +m (?) Edgar Veron

Fig. 60 Tito Crisol and Sofia Z. Villanueva and seven of their older children

Fig. 61 Front L-R: Alice, Gertrudez, Sofia, Tito, Asuncion, Soledad. Back from L-R: Adela, Marichu, Gregorio, Clemente and Gualberto. Missing: Juanito, Amalia and Rodolfo.

Note: Tito Crisol was a bookkeeper of Smith Bell & Co. The lineage of Sofia (Nena) Zulueta Villanueva and Tito Crisol was taken mostly from the Facebook 2018 posting of Marichu Crisol Reynolds, and Soledad Crisol Spangler. The rest of the information was from Angela Villanueva Rios Sr. (I).

Sources: Angela Villanueva Rios Sr. (I); Marichu Crisol Reynolds' Facebook posting; Soledad Crisol Spangler.

MVG-2.5.4. **22. Juanito Zulueta Villanueva (I)**

Note: Juanito Zulueta Villanueva (I) died single and had no issue. **End of line.**

Source: Angela Villanueva Rios Sr. (I)

MVG-2.5.5 **23. Soledad Zulueta Villanueva (I)**

Note: Soledad Zulueta Villanueva (I) died single and had no issue. **End of Line.**

Source: Angela Villanueva Rios Sr. (I)

Fig. 62 Soledad Zulueta Villanueva with her sister Sofia Villanueva Crisol and an unnamed lady at the back. Picture courtesy of Marichu Crisol Reynolds

MVG-2.5.6 **24. Carmelo Zulueta Villanueva (I)**
July 16, 1904 – (?)

CARMELO ZULUETA VILLANUEVA HAD NO ISSUE WITH +m FILOMINA SALAZAR. End of Line.

Note: Carmelo Zulueta Villanueva (I) and his wife Filomina Salazar had no issue.

Source: Angela Villanueva Rios Sr. (I); birthdate of Carmelo was given by Vicki Zulueta Antipolo of Singapore.

MVG-2.5.7 **25. Conchita Zulueta Villanueva (I)**

CHILDREN OF CONCHITA ZULUETA VILLANUEVA with +m VENANCIO BASCO OF BACACAY

MVG-2.5.7.1	1. Januario V. Basco (I) +m Dr. Noida Liboro
MVG-2.5.7.2	2. Nenita V. Basco (I) +m Atty. Paul Porcia
MVG-2.5.7.3	3. Pedro V. Basco (IV) +m Alma (?)

Note: According to Muriel De Lejos Riosa, during the Japanese occupation, they would invite Conchita Villanueva Basco to Tabaco to play mahjong and the "tong" that they would get from these weekend majhong sessions was used to buy food.

Sources: Angela Villanueva Rios Sr.(I); Muriel de Lejos Riosa (I); Facebook posting of Hector Awitin Morales Jr. (III).

MVG-2.5.8^2 **26. Roman Manjares Villanueva** (I)

CHILDREN OF ROMAN MANJARES VILLANUEVA (I) wife +m. (?)

MVG-2.5.8^2.1	1. Alfredo (?) Villanueva (I)
MVG-2.5.8^2.2	2. Milagros (?) Villanueva (I)

Note: To date no further information regarding Roman Manjares

Sources: Geni 2015 posting of Rafael Cope Villanueva from Melbourne, Australia; Antonio Morales Villanueva (VIII) telephone conversation on August 7, 2018 from California;

MVG-2.5.9^2 **27. Felipa Manjares Villanueva (I)**

CHILD OF FELIPA MAJARES VILLANUEVA with +m. RUPERTO AMBIL Sr.

MVG-2.5.9^2.1   1. Ruperto V. Ambil Jr. (I)

Note: To date, no further information regarding Felipa.

Sources: 2015 Geni posting of Rafael Cope Villanueva of Melbourne, Australia; telelphone conversation with Antonio Morales Villanueva (VIII) on August 7, 2018, Northern California.

MVG-2.5.10^2 **28. Reynaldo Manjares Villanueva Sr. (I)**

CHILD OF REYNALDO MANJARES VILLANUEVA Sr. with +m^2. "DODENG" (?)

MVG-2.5.10^2.1^2 1. Reynaldo (?) Villanueva Jr. (II)

Note: To date, no further information regarding Reynaldo Manjares Villanueva Sr..

MVG-2.5.11^2 **29. Honesto Majares Villanueva (I)**

Fig. 63 Picture of Honesto Manjares Villanueva 2nd from right standing. Picture from Dr. Audrey V. Vargas Facebook April 13, 2019 posting.

CHILDREN OF HONESTO MANJARES VILLANUEVA (I) with +m. SALVACION MORALES

MVG-2.5.11^2.1	1. Antonio M. Villanueva (VII) +m Eden Regalado
MVG-2.5.11^2.2	2. Virgilio M. Villanueva (I)
MVG-2.5.11^2.3	3. Cynthia M. Villanueva (I) single **End of Line**
MVG-2.5.11^2.4	4. Alberto Samson M. Villanueva (I) +m Dr. Berly Mauhay
MVG-2.5.11^2.5	5. Joel M. Villanueva (I)
MVG-2.5.11^2.6	6. Vivian M. Villanueva (I)
MVG-2.5.11^2.7	7. Audrey M. Villanueva (I) +m Ronaldo Caguia Vargas

Note: Honesto Manjares Villanueva (I) served as Treasurer of Tabaco. He died of heart attack.

Sources: 2016 e-mail of Rafael Cope Villanueva (III) of Melbourne, Australia; Antonio Manjares Villanueva telephone conversation of August 7, 2018 from Northern California;

MVG-2.5.12^2 **30. Amado Manjares Villanueva (I)**

CHILD OF AMADO MAJARES VILLANUEVA with +m. JOSEFA RANARA

MVG-2.5.12^2.1   1. Jaime R. Villanueva (I)

Note: To date, no further information regarding the lineage of Amado M. Villanueva (I) with Josefa Ranara.

Source: Antonio Morales Villanueva telephone conversation of August 7, 2018 from Northern California.

CHILDRENN OF AMADO MANJARES VILLANUEVA with +m^2. ANDREA ENCISA

MVG-2.5.12^2.2^2	1. Oscar E. Villanueva (I)
MVG-2.5.12^2.3^2	2. Efren E. Villanueva (I)
MVG-2.5.12^2.4^2	3. Manuel E. Villanueva (II)
MVG-2.5.12^2.5^2	4. Roberto E. Villanueva (I)
MVG-2.5.12^2.6^2	5. Lilia E. Villanueva (I)

Note: To date no further information regarding Amado M. Villanueva (I)

Source: 2015 Geni posting of Rafael Cope Manjares (III) of Melbourne, Australia

MVG-2.5.13²   **31. Evelina Manjares Villanueva**

CHILDREN OF AVELINA MANJARES VILLANUEVA (I) with +m. GUILLERMO DE LA RIVA Sr. OF CEBU.

MVG-2.5.13².1	1. Guillermo V. de la Riva Jr. (II)
MVG-2.5.13².2	2. Emilia V. de la Riva (I)
MVG-2.5.13².3	3. Rafael V. de la Riva (II)

Note: To date, no further information regarding this family.

Sources: 2015 Geni posting of Rafael Cope Villanueva (III); Hector Awitin Morales Jr. (III).

MVG-2.5.14²   **32. Gloria Manjares Villanueva**

GLORIA MANJARES VILLANUEVA AND HER HUSBAND DELFIN DE VERA HAS NO ISSUE.

Note: Gloria Manjares Villanueva and her husband +m. Delfin de Vera had no issue. **End of Line.**

Sources: 2015 Geni posting and 2016 e-mail of Rafael Cope Villanueva (III) of Melbourne, Australia.

MVG-2.5.15²   **33. Luis Manjares Villanueva (I)**

CHILDREN OF LUIS MANJARES VILLANUEVA (I) with +m. SALVACION COPE

MVG-2.5.15².1	1. Rafael C. Villanueva (III) +m Dolores Roque
MVG-2.5.15².2	2. Audrey C. Villanueva (II) +m Armi del Mundo
MVG-2.5.15².3	3. Roberto C. Villanueva (II) + Ssan Robles +m² Doris Santos
MVG-2.5.15².4	4. Maria Luisa C. Villanueva (I) +m Reymundo Ortiz
MVG-2.5.15².5.	5. Luis C. Villanueva (II) +m (?) from Thailand +m² Maylene Avorque
MVG-2.5.15².6	6. Hilario C. Villanueva (I) +m Dolores Mateo +m² Joy
MVG-2.5.15².7	7. Gloria C. Villanueva (I) +m Tony Corso
MVG-2.5.15².8	8. Armin C. Villanueva (I) TJ Wunderley +m² Maxine Ann Palad

Fig. 64 Luis M. Villanueva 90th birthday celebration in Matagbac. Hector Awitin (III) Morales Facebook august 20, 2018 posting.

Note: Luis Manjares Villanueva (I) worked at the Bureau of Custom in Tabaco, Albay with the help of Enrique Villanueva Morales (I).[1] He is now retired and lives with his wife in Matagbac, Tabaco, Albay.

Sources: [1] Conversation with Dolores Dy Alparce Morales on 4/24/2011; 2015 Geni posting and 2016 e-mail of Rafael Cope Villanueva (II) from Melbourne, Australia; 2018 Facebook posting by Villanueva relatives.

MVG-2.6.1   **34. Salvador Bautista Villanueva (I)**

Note: Salvador Bautista Villanueva died of Typhus fever. He was single. **End of Line.**

Source: Angela Villanueva Rios Sr. (I)

MVG-2.6.2   **35. Leticia Bautista Villanueva (I)**

Note: Died of old age under the care of Dolores Dy Alparce Morales 4/24/2011. She was single. **End of Line.**

Sources: Angela Villanueva Rios Sr. (I); 4/24/2011 conversation with Dolores Dy Alparce Morales.

MVG-2.6.3   **36. Mariano Bautista Villanueva (III)**

CHILDREN OF MARIANO BAUTISTA VILLANUEVA (III) with +m. ROSALINA (?)

MVG-2.6.3.1	1. Teresita (?) Villanueva (I)
MVG-2.6.3.2	2. Luz (?) Villanueva (II)
MVG-2.6.3.3	3. Grace (?) Villanueva (I)
MVG-2.6.3.4	4. Mariano (?) Villanueva (IV)
MVG-2.6.3.5	5. Helen (?) Villanueva (I)
MVG-2.6.3.6	6. Amelia (?) Villanueva
MVG-2.6.3.7	7. Steve (?) Villanueva (I) died single **End of Line.**

Note: Mariano Bautista Villanueva was known as "WoWo". His children were raised by his sister, Erlinda Villanueva Glazer at her house in Mandaluyong while he stayed at her summerhouse in San Lorenzo, Tabaco, Albay with his common law wife. No further information with regards to his children with his common law wife.

Sources: Common knowledge. The complete list of his children were from the 2018 Facebook posting of Hector Awitin Morales Jr. (III)

MVG-2.6.4   **37. Raul Bautista Villanueva (I)**

Note: No further information regarding the lineage of Raul Bautista Villanueva (I) except that he was a dentist and that he moved to Mindanao. According to the 2018 Facebook posting of Hector Awitin Morales, he moved to Zamboanga.

Sources: Angela Villanueva Rios Sr. (I); 2018 Facebook posting of Hector Awitin Morales Jr. (III)

MVG-2.6.5   **38. Erlinda Bautista Villanueva (I)**

CHILD OF ERLINDA BAUTISTA VILLANUEVA with +n.m. Dr. TURLA OF PAMPANGA

MVG-2.6.5.1   1. Antonio (Dario?) B. Villanueva (VII) single **End of Line.**

ERLINDA BAUTISTA VILLANUEVA HAD NO ISSUE with +m. CHARLES GLAZER.

Note: During the Japanese occupation, Erlinda Bautista Villanueva had a run-in with the law and spent a short time in prison. Later, she was helped and hired by the wife of President Roxas who was a relative of Erlinda's mother, Consuelo. Erlinda worked as housekeeper and interior decorator of Malacañang Palace.

According to Angela Villanueva Rios Sr.(I), the son of Erlinda Bautista Villanueva with Dr. Turla of Pampanga was named Antonio and he was called by his nickname, Pocholo, by relatives. However, in his obituary his name was listed as Dario.

Erlinda in her later years married Charles Glazer who was the CIA Director of the Philippines at the time. Antonio (Dario ?) Villanueva was later adopted by Charles Glazer on one condition that he behaves and cause no trouble to dishonor the family.

Erlinda Bautista Villanueva (I) and Charles Glazer had no issue.

Sources: Angela Villanueva Rios Sr (I); 2018 Facebook posting of Dario (Antonio?) Villanueva's obituary.

MVG-2.6.6   **39. Consuelo Bautista Villanueva Jr. (I)**

CHILDREN OF CONSUELO BAUTISTA VILLANUEVA with +m. MELQUIEDES TORRES Sr.

MVG-2.6.6.1   1. Carmen V. Torres (I) +m Vicente Go
MVG-2.6.6.2   2. Pedro V. Torres (VI) +m Basilisa Andes
MVG-2.6.6.3   3. Melquiedes V. Torres Jr. (I) +n.m. (?)
MVG-2.6.6.4   4. Elvira V. Torres (II) +m Thomas McNamara
MVG-2.6.6.5   5. Rosario V. Torres (I) +m Aldo Cordia

Note: The lineage of theTorres family was from Mrs. Consuelo Villanueva Torres Jr. (II) who was visited by Angela V. Rios Howe Jr. (III) at the house of Consuelo's daughter Elvira McNamara in Southern California.

Source: Mrs. Consuelo Villanueva Torres Sr. (I). Correction of the family name of "Torres" was given by Elvira Torres McNamara 4/5/2019, "Familia Villanueva de Tabaco"; also by Rebecca Quijano 4/5/19.

Fig. 65 Consuelo Villanueva Torres. Picture courtesy of Jacob Go Facebook posting 2018.

Fig. 66 From L-R: Magin E. Riosa Jr., Erlinda V. Glazer, Leticia B.Villanueva, Mariano B.Villanueva Jr. Back row L-R: Carmencho Go, (?), Santiago E. Riosa (?). Picture from Toti Quijano's Facebook posting July 7, 2013.

MVG-2.8.1 **40. Fermin Ante Villanueva (I)**

CHILDREN OF FERMIN ANTE VILLANUEVA (I) with +m. ANITA(?)

MVG-2.8.1.1   1. Eddie (?) Villanueva (I)
MVG-2.8.1.2   2. Rosie (?) Villanueva (I)

FERMIN ANTE VILLANUEVA +m^2 "LALENG" HAD NO ISSUE. END OF LINE.

Note: Fermin Ante Villanueva had told Orestes Murillo Morales information regarding Mariano P. Villanueva Sr. (I), which are included in the introduction of this Genealogy and also in Chapter II.

    "Laleng" was the mistress of Andres Ty Rios. Angela V. Rios Sr. (I) said that Fermin was matched and convinced to marry "Laleng" by Jesus Salvador Blance Rios Sr., to get Salvador's father, Andres Ty Rios, away from "Laleng".

    Orestes said that Fermin used to wear and show off the expensive ring that Andres Ty Rios gave "Laleng".

Sources: Angela Villaueva Rios Sr. (I); convesation with Orestes Murillo Morales and Dolores Dy Alparce Morales on 4/24/2011 while visiting California; conversation on March 19, 2019 with Carlos Manuel V. Rios Sr. (I) at his house in La Verne, California.

MVG-2.8.2   **41. Sigfredo Ante Villanueva (I)**

CHILDREN OF SIGFREDO ANTE VILLANUEVA with +m. MERCEDEZ PARCIA

MVG-2.8.2.1   1. Antonia P. Villanueva (I)
MVG-2.8.2.2   2. Sylvia P. Villanueva (I)

Note: Angela Villanueva Rios Sr. (I) gave the lineage of the Ante family but did not mention Sigrfredo. Annie Riosa Nañoz and Hector Awitin Morales Jr. (III) had mentioned him and his family at their Facebook postings under "Familia Villanueva de Tabaco".

Source: Angela Villanueva Rios Sr. (I); Annie Riosa Nañoz; 2018 Facebook posting of Hector Awitin Morales Jr. (III).

MVG-2.8.3   **42. Dominador Ante Villanueva (I)**
CHILDREN OF DOMINADOR ANTE VILLANUEVA with +m. JUANA LOMIBAO

MVG-2.8.3.1   1. Carmelita L. Villanueva (I)
MVG-2.8.3.2   2. Arturo L. Villanueva (I)
MVG-2.8.3.3   3. Grace L. Villanueva (I)

Note: There is no further information as to Dominador Ante Villanueva's wife. Annie Riosa Nañoz confirmed the names of the children of Dominador Ante Villanueva on her 10/24/18 Facebook posting.

Sources: Angela Villanueva Rios (I); Facebook posting "Familia Villanueva de Tabaco"; 2018 Facebook posting of Hector Awitin Morales Jr. (III); Annie Riosa Nañoz.

MVG-2.8.4   **43. Adelaida Ante Villanueva (I)**

ADELAIDA ANTE VILLANUEVA with +m/s JUAN NICOLAS **HAD NO ISSUE. END OF LINE.**

Fig. 67 Adelaida Ante Villanueva. Picture courtesy of Corina Belle Villar

Fig. 68 Adelaida Villanueva Nicolas through the years. Pictures courtesy of Corina Belle Riosa Villar.

Fig. 69 Adelaida V. Nicolas held a birthday party in honor of her nephew, Magin Riosa Jr. on April 24, 1953 (?) Front: Hector Quijano Jr. Starting from 2nd row as numbered from L-R: 1) Luisito Revaya 2) Luisito Kare 3) Eddie Villanueva 4) Magin Riosa Jr. 5) Pedring Alegria 6) Orestes Morales 7) Rene Kare 8) Noel Mirasol 9) Florino Sevilla 10) Fe Bocalbos 11) Ruth Sanchez 12) Rosie Villanueva 13) Adelaida V. Nicolas 14) Josefina Manalang Quijano 15) Melania Demetrio 16) Henrietta Abundo 17) Clemente

Crisol 18) David Abundo 19) Eva Cruel 20) Salvacion Demetrio 21) Romulo Abundo 22) Aristedis Demetrio 23) Purita Riosa 24) Catrina Demetrio 25) Cely Kare 26) Romulo Villar 27) Paito Abrigo.

Note: Adelaida Ante Villanueva had no issue with her husband Juan Nicolas, a journalist from Ligao (?). They separated and according to Patricia R. Wood, she became the mistress of a very influential politician who gave her a stipend for life. She spent most of her life with the family of her aunt Francisca Arana Villanueva Riosa and cousin Dr. Magin V. Riosa Sr. (I). To pass the time, she played *entre cuatro* and majhong with relatives.

Sources: Angela Villanueva Rios Sr. (I); common knowledge; Conversation with Carlos Manuel V. Rios Sr. (I) on 3/19/2019 at his house in La Verne, California; Patricia R. Wood.

MVG-2.8.5   **44. Carlito Ante Villanueva (I)**

Note: To date, no further information regarding Carlito's lineage. Robert Lianco gave the first name of Carlito Ante Villanueva's wife – "Mila"

Source: Angela Villanueva Rios Sr. (I); Robert Lianco

MVG-2.8.6   **45. Delfin Ante Villanueva Jr. (II)**

CHILDREN OF DELFIN ANTE VILLANUEVA JR, with +m HERMINIA CHAVEZ

MVG-2.8.6.1   1. Sonia C. Villanueva (I)
MVG-2.8.6.2   2. Merle C. Villanueva (I)
MVG-2.8.6.3   3. Dr. Maribel C. Uichanco (I)
MVG-2.8.6.4   4. Dr. Angela C. Villanueva (IV)

Note: This posting of Dr. Maribel Villanueva Uichanco was reposted by Annie Riosa Nañoz on 10/24/18 for this Genealogical Record.

Sources: Dr. Maribel Villanueva Uichanco; Annie Riosa Nañoz.

MVG-2.9.1   **46. Catalina Villanueva Morales (I)**

CHILDREN OF CATALINA VILLANUEVA MORALES with +m JOSÉ DE LUNA GONZALES

MVG-2.9.1.1	1. Carmita M. Gonzales (I)
MVG-2.9.1.2	2. Mila M. Gonzales (I)
MVG-2.9.1.3	3. José (Pepito) M. Gonzales Jr. (V)

Note: Angela Villanueva Rios Sr. (I) claimed that Catalina is an "Hija natural" although of whom was not clarified. She also said that Catalina had suggested to Quiteria Villanueva, during the (Filipino - American War?) to take out the jewelries being kept at Monte de Piedad and put them in her safe keeping. After the War Catalina refused to return the jewelries to Quiteria. There was a time, due to finacial hardship, the Morales family had to live at the house of Pedro and Quiteria Villanueva.

Sources: Common knowledge among Quiteria's children; Angela Villanueva Rios Sr. (I); The names of the children of Catalina Morales Villanueva were from the 2018 Facebook posting of Hector Awitin Morales Jr. (III); Robert Lianco.

MVG-2.9.2.   **47. Natalia Villanueva Morales (I)**

Note: To date, there is no information regarding Natalia except that she was single according to Angela V. Rios Sr. (I)

Sources: Angela Villanueva Rios Sr. (I); Robert Lianco; Hector Awitin Morales Jr. (III).

MVG-2.9.3   **48. Ramon Villanueva Morales (I)**

CHILDREN OF RAMON VILLANUEVA MORALES with +m VISITACION VILLANUEVA

MVG-2.9.3.1	1. Lorenzo V. Morales (I)
MVG-2.9.3.2	2. Teresita V. Morales (II)

Note: To date, no further information regarding Ramon V. Morales and his family.

Sources: 12/1/2015 e-mail of Robert Lianco of Tabaco; 2018 Facebook posting of Hector Awitin Morales Jr. (III)

MVG-2.9.4   **49. Enrique Villanueva Morales (I)**

CHILDREN OF ENRIQUE MORALES WITH HIS WIFE TRINIDAD MURILLO

MVG-2.9.4.1   1. Orestes M. Morales (I) +m Dolores Dy Alparce
MVG-2.9.4.2   2. Evelina M. Morales (I) + m Agustin Bufarull
MVG-2.9.4.3   3. Hector M. Morales (II) +m Morina Awitin
MVG-2.9.4.4   4. Edgardo M. Morales (I) +m Teresita Regalado
MVG-2.9.4.5   5. Linden M. Morales (I) +m Marilyn Medrano +m^2
                      Bernardine de los Reyes

Fig. 70 Enrique Morales. Picture courtesy of Hector Awitin Morales Jr. (III)

Fig. 71 Picture courtesy of Hector Awitin Morales Jr. (III) Facebook posting at the "Familia Villanueva de Tabaco".

Note: Dolores Dy Alparce Morales had given the lineage of the Morales family on 4/24/2011 on their visit to California.

Sources: (Ting) Orestes Murillo Morales and Dolores Dy Alparce Morales on their 4/24/2011 visit to California; Hector Awitin Morales Jr. (III) 2018 Facebook posting.

Fig. 72 Turn Over Ceremony. Enrique Villanueva Morales as Chief of Police, District of Manila. Picture courtesy of Hector Awitin Morales Jr. (III) Facebook posting at "Familia Villanueva de Tabaco."

MVG-2.9.5 **50. Luz (Nening) Villanueva Morales (I)**

Note: Luz or Nening was single and she died of old age under the care of Dolores Dy Alparce Morales.

Sources: Angela Villanueva Rios (I); Dolores (Dy) Alparce Morales

MVG-2.9.6 **51. Lourdes (Nenita) Villanueva Morales (I)**

CHILDREN OF NENITA VILLANUEVA MORALES with +m BENITO SERRANO

MVG-2.9.6.1	1. Antonio M. Serrano
MVG-2.9.6.2	2. "Cheling" M. Serrano
MVG-2.9.6.3	3. "Loling" M. Serrano
MVG-2.9.6.4	4. "Chito" M. Serrano

Note: There had been confusion as to the lineage of the Serrano family. The children's names were taken from Hector Awitin Morales Jr. (III) Facebook posting.

Sources: Angela Villanueva Rios (I); Patricia Rios Wood; Robert Lianco; Hector Awitin Morales Jr. (III)

MVG-2.9.7 **52. Teodora Villanueva Morales (II)**

CHILDREN OF TEODORA VILLANUEVA MORALES with +m RICARDO SIKAT Sr.

MVG-2.9.7.1	1. Antonio M. Sikat
MVG-2.9.7.2	2. Miguel M. Sikat
MVG-2.9.7.3	3. Lolita M. Sikat (I) (entered a convent)
MVG-2.9.7.4	4. Ricardo M. Sikat Jr.
MVG-2.9.7.5	5. "Tata" M. Sikat
MVG-2.9.7.6	6. Sally M. Sikat

Note: Both Robert Lianco and Hector Morales Jr. (IV) mentioned "Teodora" and they both wrote that she was married to Ricardo Sikat. No further information available for this line.

Sources: Angela Villanueva Rios (I); Robert Lianco; Hector Morales Jr. (III).

MVG-2.10.1 **53. Rita (?) Villanueva (I)**

Note: No other available information regarding Rita (?) Villanueva and her husband Dr. Gonzales.

Source: Angela Villanueva Rios (I)

MVG-2.10.2 **54. Antonio (?) Villanueva (III)**

Note: No other available information regarding Antonio (?) Villanueva (III)

Source: Angela Villanueva Rios (I)

MVG-2.11.1 **55 Felix Quijano Jr. (II)**

CHILDREN OF FELIX QUIJANO (II) with +m MERCEDEZ MADRID OF TABACO

MVG-2.11.1.1   1. Jude M. Quijano

Note: According to Andres Villanueva Rios, Felix Quijano Jr. (II) refused to acknowledge being a relative of the Villanueva.

Sources: 2018 Facebook posting of Hector Awitin Morales Jr. (III); Robert Lianco; Andres Villanueva Rios (I).

MVG-2.11.2 **56. Teodoro Quijano (I)**

CHILDREN OF TEODORO QUIJANO with +m LORENA MARTINEZ

Note: According to Hector Awitin Morales Jr. (III) they have seven children. To date, there is no further available information regarding this family.

Source: Hector Awitin Morales Jr. (III)

MVG-2.11.3 **57. Angela Quijano Villanueva (II)**

CHILDREN OF ANGELA QUIJANO VILLANUEVA with +n.m. MONTEALEGRE OF TABACO

MVG-2.11.3.1	1. Victor V. Montealegre (II)
MVG-2.11.3.2	2. Miguel V. Montealegre (I)
MVG-2.11.3.3	3. Eugene V. Montealegre (I)
MVG-2.11.3.4	4. Jessica V. Montealegre (I)

Note: Angela Quijano Villanueva, was said to have been adopted by Isidora Arana Villanueva, hence she carried the Villanueva family name instead of Quijano. It is not known whether she was legally adopted or not.

She used to work for Montealegre and later became his mistress. They had several children together and whether he married her later is also unknown.

Sources: Common knowledge; Angela Villanueva Rios Sr.(I); Hector Awitin Morales Jr. (III) 2018 Facebook posting; Robert Lianco.

MVG-2.12.1 **58. Ernestina Quijano Salcedo**

CHILDREN OF ERNESTINA QUIJANO SALCEDO with +m (?) BAUTISTA

MVG-2.12.1.1   1. Bremel S. Bautista (I)
MVG-2.12.1.2   2. Pipon S. Bautista

Note: The names of the the children of Ernestina Quijano Salcedo with (?) Bautista was taken from the 2018 Facebook Posting of Hector Awitin Morales Jr. (III).

Source: Hector Awitin Morales Jr. (III)

MVG-2.12.2 **59. Enrique Quijano Salcedo (II)**

Note: According to Hector Awitin Morales Jr. (III), Enrique Quijano Salcedo married "Nena" Picaso of Manila. To date, no other available information regarding this family.

Source: Hector Awitin Morales Jr. (III)

MVG-2.13.1 **60. Hector Abraham Quijano (I)**

Fig. 73 Hector Quijano Sr. Picture from Toti Quijano's Facebook posting om June 8, 2011

Fig. 74 Hector Abraham Quijano and his family. Front row from L-R: Ricardo, Jose, Hector Sr., Josefina, Felipe, Antonio; back row from L-R: Jocelyn, Rebecca, Edgardo Ulpindo, Cielo, Hector Jr., Mario, Julio. Picture courtesy of Mario Manalang Quijano (I).

CHILDREN OF HECTOR ABRAHAM QUIJANO (I) with +m JOSEFINA MANALANG OF TABACO

MVG-2.13.1.1	1. Cielo M. Quijano (I) +m Edgardo Ulpindo
MVG-2.13.1.2	2. Hector M. Qujano Jr. (II) +m Pacita Mendoza
MVG-2.13.1.3	3. Mario M. Quijano +m. Cecilia Tambunting Quijano
MVG-2.13.1.4.	4. Rebecca M. Qujano (I) +m/s Jun Nagaoka
MVG-2.13.1.5	5. Julio M. Quijano (II) +m Genevie Ang
MVG-2.13.1.6	6. Joselyn M. Quijano (I) +m Valerio Kalaw
MVG-2.13.1.7	7. José M. Quijano +m Elizabeth de Asis
MVG-2.13.1.8	8. Ricardo M. Quijano +m Gina Bagasan
MVG-2.13.1.9	9. Felipe M. Quijano +m Rosanna Almeda
MVG-2.13.1.10	10. Antonio M. Quijano +m Joan Co

Note: Based on the telephone conversation with Antonio Morales Villanueva (VI), on 8/7/18, he claimed that Hector Quijano was the stepson of Julio Quijano. According to him, Hector had admitted as much that he was the stepson of Julio Quijano at the reunion of the Villanueva relatives in San Roque when Enrique Villanueva Morales was planning to run for Congressman.

According to Antonio, Hector cried that he could not support Enrique because he had promised to support Tecla Ziga.

There had been efforts to find corroborating statement to support this claim and had been unsuccessful so far because most of the old relatives have died already. Hector Abraham Quijano Sr. is still included in this genealogy until he is proven that he is not a blood relative.

Hector Sr. was born on August 4, 1923. He worked closely with the Ziga family in politics and was the executive secretary of congressman Venancio Ziga. Through Ziga, he was given work at ABACORP.

During the Martial Law, Hector was arrested by the CIS and jailed for supposedly some kind of business deal that went awry. He was found dead hanging on his cell on January 28, 1981. The authorities claimed he committed suicide. There was no formal investigation regarding his death and even if there was one nothing came out of it. Most of the authorities involved in his case are no longer around.

His wife, Josefina Manalang Quijano was born March 16, 1924 and died of old age on October 27, 2013 in Northern California.

Mario Manalang Quijano of Northern California contributed the information, pictures and names of the children of Hector Abraham Quijano and their respective spouses. Complete list of spouses was sent 4/5/2019, 5:22 A.M. The information regarding the circumstances of his death was sent through text on May 12, 2019.

Sources: Angela Villanueva Rios Sr. (I); 8/7/18 telephone conversation with Antonio Morales Villannueva; Mario Manalang Quijano (I) (9/19/2018) visit to Santa Maria, California and 4/5/2019; 5/12/19 texts.

Fig. 75 2018 Lunch gathering of some of the Villanueva families at Mall of Asia, Metro Manila, Philippines

Chapter IV

LIST OF VILLANUEVA FAMILIES BY GENERATION

FIRST GENERATION:

1. Villanueva, Vicente (I)
2. Villanueva, Mariano Porferio (I)

SECOND GENERATION:

VICENTE P. VILLANUEVA (I) +n.m. MABIHIS LINE

1. Villanueva, Quiteria Mabihis (I)
2. Villanueva, Maria Mabihis (I)
3. Villanueva, Antonio Mabihis (I)

VICENTE P. VILLANUEVA (I) +m. (?) TOMAS LINE

1. **Villanueva, Balbino Tomas (I)**

MARIANO P. VILLANUEVA SR. (I) +m TEODORA ARANA LINE

1. Villanueva, Pedro Arana Sr. (I)
2. Riosa, Francisca Villanueva (I)
3. Liangco, Maria Villanueva (II)
4. Villanueva, Antonio Arana (II)
5. Villanueva, Rafael Arana (I)
6. Villanueva, Mariano Arana Sr. (II)
7. Villanueva, Isidora Arana (I)
8. Villanueva, Delfin Arana (I)
9. Morales, Candida Villanueva (I)
10. Villanueva, Vicente Arana (II)

MARIANO P. VILLANUEVA SR. (I) +n.m. "LANYANG" QUIJANO LINE

11. Quijano, Felix (I)
12. Quijano, Julio (I)
13. Salcedo, Melania Quijano (I)
14. Siquia, Toribia Quijano (I)

MARIANO P. VILLANUEVA SR. +n.m. UNNAMED LADY LINE

15. Villanueva, Maria (III)

MARIANO P. VILLANUEVA SR. (I) +n.m. QUITERIA BUENCONSEJO LINE

16. Villanueva, Balbino Buenconsejo (II)

THIRD GENERATION:

PEDRO ARANA VILLANUEVA Sr. +m QUITERIA VILLANUEVA LINE

1. Villanueva, Dr. Vicente Luis Villanueva (III)
2. Villanueva, Felicidad Villanueva (I)
3. Santos, Leonor Villanueva (I)
4. De Lejos, Remedios Villanueva (I)
5. Villanueva, PedroVillanueva Jr. (II)
6. Villanueva, Daria Villanueva (I)
7. Villanueva, José Villanueva (I)
8. Rios, Angela Villanueva Sr. (I)

PEDRO ARANA VILLANUEVA WITH +n.m. MIRASOL LINE

9. Mirasol, Adriano Sr. (Villanueva) (I)

FRANCISCA ARANA VILLANUEVA +m. SANTIAGO RIOSA LINE

1. Solano, Pilar Riosa (I)
2. Calleja, Consolacion Riosa (I)
3. Riosa, Magin Villanueva Sr. (I)

MARIA ARANA VILLANUEVA +m. IGNACIO LIANGCO (Sr.) LINE

1. Almonte, Socorro Liangco (I)
2. Liangco, Luzon (Ignacio Jr. ?) Villanueva (I?)
3. Liangco, Amparo Villanueva (I)
4. Ontinero, Felicidad Liangco (II)

ANTONIO ARANA VILLANUEVA Sr. +m. TERESITA (?) OF SPAIN LINE

1. Villanueva, Antonio Jr. (?) (III)
2. Villanueva, Pedro (?) (III)

RAFAEL ARANA VILLANUEVA Sr.+m. MARIQUITA ZULUETA LINE

1. Almonte, Trinidad Villanueva (I)
2. Villanueva, Rafaelito Zulueta Jr. (II)
3. Crisol, Sofia Villanueva (I)

4. Villanueva Juanito Zulueta (I)
5. Villanueva, Soledad Zulueta (I)
6. Villanueva, Carmelo Zulueta (I)
7. Basco, Conchita Villanueva (I)

RAFAEL ARANA VILLANUEVA +m.^{2} FLAVIANA MANJARES LINE

1. Villanueva, Roman Manjares (I)
2. Ambil, Felipa Villanueva (I)
3. Villanueva, Reynaldo Manjares (I)
4. Villanueva, Honesto Manjares (I)
5. Villanueva, Amado Manjares (I)
6. De La Riva, Avelina Villanueva (I)
7. De Vera, Gloria Villanueva (I)
8. Villanueva, Luis Manjares (I)

MARIANO ARANA VILLANUEVA Sr. +m. CONSUELO REANZARES BAUTISTA LINE

1. Villanueva, Salvador Bautista (I)
2. Villanueva, Leticia Bautista (I)
3. Villanueva, Mariano Jr. Bautista (III)
4. Villanueva, Raul Bautista (I)
5. Glazer, Erlinda Villanueva (I)
6. Torres, Consuelo Jr. Villanueva (I)

DELFIN ARANA VILLANUEVA Sr. +m. TELESFORA ANTE LINE

1. Villanueva, Fermin Ante (I)
2. Villanueva, Sigfredo Ante (I)
3. Villanueva, Dominador Ante (I)
4. Nicolas, Adelaida Villanueva (I)
5. Villanueva, Carlito Ante (I)
6. Villanueva, Delfin Jr. Ante (II)

CANDIDA ARANA VILLANUEVA +m. RAMON MORALES LINE

1. Gonzales, Catalina Morales (I)
2. Morales, Natalia Villanueva (I)
3. Morales, Ramon Jr. Villanueva (I)
4. Morales, Enrique Villanueva (I)
5. Serrano, Luz Morales (I)
6. Morales Lourdez Villanueva (I)
7. Sikat, Teodora Morales (I)

VICENTE ARANA VILLANUEVA +m. "TINAY" (?) LINE

1. Villanueva, Rita (?) (I)
2. Villanueva, Antonio (?) (IV)

FELIX QUIJANO Sr. +m. MAXIMA BUALOY LINE

1. Quijano, Felix Jr. Bualoy (I)
2. Quijano, Teodoro Bualoy (I)
3. Quijano, Angela (II)

MELANIA QUIJANO +m. (?) SALCEDO LINE

1. Bautista, Ernestina Salcedo (I)
2. Salcedo, Enrique Quijano (II)

JULIO QUIJANO +m. ROSARIO ABRAHAM LINE

1. Quijano, Hector Abraham (I) (?)

FOURTH GENERATION:

DR. VICENTE VILLANUEVA VILLANUEVA Sr. +m. AUREA PATO LINE

1. Villanueva, Vicente Pato Jr. (IV)
2. Guinto, Paz Villanueva (I)
3. Albarico, Celia Villanueva (I)

LEONOR VILLANUEVA VILLANUEVA +m. JOSÉ DIAZ SANTOS LINE

1. Tuaño, Josefina Santos (I)
2. Santos, Celia Villanueva (II)
3. Duria, Erlinda Nieves Santos (II)

REMEDIOS VILLANUEVA VILLANUEVA +m. FRANCISCO DE LEJOS Sr. LINE

1. Buenconsejo, Margarita de Lejos (I)
2. De Lejos, Francisco Jr. Villanueva (II)
3. Riosa, Muriel de Lejos (I)
4. De Lejos, Luz Villanueva (II)
5. Pleta, Sofia Remedios de Los Angeles de Lejos (I)

DARIA VILLANUEVA VILLANUEVA +n.m. LUIS MADRID LINE

1. Villanueva, Antonio (Madrid) (V)

PEDRO VILLANUEVA VILLANUEVA Jr. +n.m. UNNAMED WOMAN FROM LEGASPI LINE

1. Garcia, Elvira Villanueva (I)

JOSE VILLANUEVA VILLANUEVA Sr. (I) +n.m. (?) ELEUTERIA BOBIS LINE

1. Jaymalin, Conchita Villanueva (II)
2. Villanueva Eduardo Bobis (I)
3. Villanueva, José Bobis Jr. (II)
4. Villanueva, Pedro Bobis (III)
5. Patiag, Teresa Villanueva (I)
6. Pingol, Gloria Natividad Villanueva (I)
7. Gumabao, Fe Nancy Villanueva (I)
8. Moran, Rosemarie Joy Villanueva (I)

ANGELA VILLANUEVA VILLANUEVA +m. JESUS SALVADOR BLANCE RIOS LINE

1. Wood, Maria Leticia Patricia Rios (I)
2. Rios, José Villanueva (III)
3. Rios, Juanito Salvador Villanueva Sr. (I)
4. Diño, Emma Victoria Palomar (legally adopted by Guadioso Palomar and Flora Rios Palomar) (I)
5. Rios, Carlos Manuel Sr. Villanueva (I)
6. Kare, Maria Teresa Concepcion Rios (I)
7. Rios, Jaime Miguel Villanueva (I)
8. Howe, Angela Rios (III)
9. Rios, Andres Villanueva (I)
10. Rios, Cesar Antonio Villanueva (I)

ADRIANO MIRASOL Sr. (VILLANUEVA) +m. ASUNCION BARBANTE LINE

1. Mirasol, Manuel Barbante (I)
2. De la Cruz, Fe Mirasol (I)
3. Mirasol, Ramon Barbante (II)
4. Mirasol, Adriano Jr. Barbante (II)
5. Mirasol, Willie May Barbante (I)
6. Mirasol Arniel Barbante (I)
7. Mirasol, Nemei (adopted)

PILAR VILLANUEVA RIOSA +m. DR. MELITON SOLANO LINE

1. Solano, Hector Riosa (II)

DR. MAGIN VILLANUEVA RIOSA SR. (Dentist) +n.m. LAYOG LINE

1. Riosa, Mario Layog (I)
2. Riosa, Emma Layog (I)
3. Riosa (?) Layog

DR. MAGIN VILLANUEVA RIOSA SR. (Dentist) +m. PURIFICACION ESTEVEZ LINE

1. Castro, Pilar Riosa (II)
2. Bruselas, Ester Riosa (I)
3. Nañoz, Adela Riosa (I)
4. Riosa, Santiago Estevez (I)
5. Ala, Josefina Riosa (II)
6. Riosa, Magin Estevez Jr. (II)
7. Peña, Purita Riosa (I)

LUZON (IGNACIO?) LIANGCO (Jr. ?) +m. (?) LINE

1. Liangco, Francisca (?) (II)

SOCORRO VILLANUEVA LIANGCO +m. MARCIAL ALMONTE Sr. LINE

1. Almonte, Edgar Liangco (I)
2. Almonte, Eleanor Liangco (I)
3. Almonte, Marcial Liangco (I)

FELICIDAD VILLANUEVA LIANGCO +m GERONIMO ORTINERO Sr. LINE

1. Ortinero, Antonio Liangco (VI)
2. Ortinero, Teresita Liangco (I)
3. Ortinero, Geronimo Jr. Liangco (I)
4. Ortinero, Danilo Liangco (I)
5. Ortinero, Malou Liangco (I)
6. Ortinero, Eric Liangco (I)
7. Ortinero, Meyin Liangco (I)

TRINIDAD ZULUETA VILLANUEVA +m. DOMINGO ALMONTE LINE

1. Almonte, Lourdes Villanueva (II)
2. Almonte, Mariano Villanueva (IV)
3. Almonte, Antonio Villanueva (VII)
4. Almonte, Maria Villanueva (IV)
5. Valenzuela, Teresita Almonte (II)
6. Almonte, Soledad Villanueva (II)

SOFIA ZULUETA VILLANUEVA +m TITO CRISOL LINE

1. Crisol, Juanito Villanueva (II)
2. Alpasan, Amalia Crisol (I)
3. Crisol, Rodolfo Villanueva (I)
4. Adornado, Adela Crisol (II)
5. Reynolds, Marichu Crisol (I)
6. Crisol, Gregorio Villanueva (I)
7. Crisol, Clemente Villanueva (I)
8. Crisol, Gualberto, Villanueva (I)
9. Spangler, Soledad Crisol (III)
10. Cooper, Asuncion Crisol (I)
11. Bautista, Gertrudez Crisol (I)
12. Veron, Alice Crisol (I)

CONCHITA ZULUETA VILLANUEVA +m. VENANCIO BASCO LINE

1. Basco, Juanario Villanueva (I)
2, Porcia, Nenita Basco (I)
3, Basco Pedro Villanueva (IV)

ROMAN MANJARES VILLANUEVA +m. (?) LINE

1. Villanueva, Alfredo (?) (I)
2. Villanueva, Milagros (?) (I)

FELIPA MANJARES VILLANUEVA +m. RUPERTO AMBIL Sr. LINE

1. Ambil, Ruperto Villanueva Jr. (I)

HONESTO MANJARES VILLANUEVA +m. SALVACION MORALES LINE

1. Villanueva, Antonio Morales (VIII)
2. Villanueva, Virgilio Morales (I)
3. Villanueva, Cynthia Morales (I)
4. Villanueva, Dr. Alberto Samson Morales (I)
5. Villanueva, Joel Morales (I)
6. Villanueva Vivian Morales (I)
7. Vargas, Dr. Audrey Villanueva (Dentist) (I)

REYNALDO MANJARES VILLANUEVA Sr. +m^2 "DODENG" LINE

1. Villanueva, Reynaldo Jr. (?) (II)

AMADO MANJARES VILLANUEVA +m. JOSEFA RANARA LINE

1. Villanueva, Jaime Ranara (I)

AMADO MANJARES VILLANUEVA +m^2 ANDREA ENCISA LINE

1. Villanueva, Oscar Encisa (I)
2. Villanueva, Efren Encisa (I)
3. Villanueva, Manuel Encisas (II)
4. Villanueva, Roberto Encisa (I)
5. Villanueva, Lilia Encisa (I)

EVELINA MANJARES VILLANUEVA +m GUILLERMO DE LA RIVA Sr. LINE

1. De la Riva, Guillermo Jr. Villanueva (I)
2. De la Riva, Emelia Villanueva (I)
3. De la Riva, Rafael Villanueva (III)

LUIS MANJARES VILLANUEVA Sr. +m SALVACION COPE LINE

1. Villanueva, Rafael Cope (IV)
2. Del Mundo, Audrey Villanueva (II)
3. Villanueva, Roberto Cope (II)
4. Ortiz, Maria Luisa Villanueva (I)
5. Villanueva, Luis Cope Jr. (II)
6. Villanueva, Hilario Cope (I)
7. Corso, Gloria Villanueva (I)
8. Villanueva, Armin Cope (I)

MARIANO BAUTISTA VILLANUEVA Jr/ Sr. +m. ROSALINA SANTOS LINE

1. Villanueva, Teresita Santos (III)
2. Villanueva, Luz Santos (III)
3. Villanueva, Grace Santos (I)
4. Villanueva, Mariano Santos Jr. (V)
5. Villanueva, Helen Santos (I)
6. Villanueva, Amelia Santos (I)
7. Villanueva, Steve Santos (I)

ERLINDA BAUTISTA VILLANUEVA +n.m. DR. TURLA OF PAMPANGA LINE

1. Glazer, Antonio Dario Villanueva (Adopted by Charles Glazer) (I)

CONSUELO BAUTISTA VILLANUEVA Jr. +m. MELQUEIDEZ TORRES Sr. LINE

1. Go, Carmen Torres (I)
2. Torres, Pedro Villanueva (V)
3. Torres, Melqueidez Villanueva Jr. (I)
4. McNamara, Elvira Torres (I)

5. Cordia, Rosario Torres (I)

FERMIN ANTE VILLANUEVA AND +m. ANITA (?) LINE

1. Villanueva, Eddie (?) (I)
2. Villanueva, Rosie (?) (I)

SIGFREDO ANTE VILLANUEVA + m. MERCEDEZ PARCIA LINE

1. Wilson, Antonia Villanueva (I)
2. Reyes, Sylvia Villanueva (I)

DOMINADOR ANTE VILLANUEVA +m. JUANA LOMIBAO LINE

1. Villanueva, Carmelita Lomibao (I)
2. Villanueva, Arturo Lomibao (I)
3. Villanueva, Grace Lomibao (II)

DELFIN ANTE VILLANUEVA Jr. +m. HERMINIA CHAVEZ LINE

1. Villanueva, Sonia Chavez (I)
2. Reyes, Merle Villanueva (I)
3. Uichanco, Dr. Maribel Villanueva (I)
4. Villanueva, Dr. Angela Chavez (IV)

CATALINA VILLAUEVA MORALES +m JOSÉ DE LUNA GONZALES Sr. LINE

1. Asis, Carmita Gonzales (I)
2. Gonzales, Mila Morales (I)
3. Gonzales, José Morales (IV)

RAMON VILLANUEVA MORALES +m VISITACION VILLANUEVA LINE

1. Morales, Lorenzo Villanueva (I)
2. Azul, Teresita Morales (IV)

ENRIQUE VILLANUEVA MORALES +m. TRINIDAD MURILLO LINE

1. Morales, Orestes Murillo (I)
2. Bofarull, Evelina Morales (I)
3. Morales, Hector Murillo Sr. (II)
4. Morales, Edgardo Murillo (I)
5. Morales, Linden Murillo (I)

NENITA VILLANUEVA MORALES +m BENITO SERRANO LINE

1. Serrano, Antonio Morales (IX)
2. Serrano, "Cheling" Morales
3. Serrano, "Loleng" Morales
4. Serrano, "Chito Morales

TEODORA VILLANUEVA MORALES +m ATTY. RICARDO SIKAT Sr. LINE

1. Sikat, Antonio Morales (X)
2. Sikat, Miguel Morales (I)
3. Sikat, Lolita Morales (I)
4. Sikat, Ricardo Morales Jr. (I)
5. Fernandez, "Tata" Sikat
6. Agaton, Sally Sikat

FELIX QUIJANO Jr. +m MERCEDEZ MADRID LINE

1. Quijano, Jude Madrid (I)

ANGELA QUIJANO VILLANUEVA +n.m. (?) MONTEALEGRE LINE

1. Montealegre, Victor Villanueva (II)
2. Montealegre, Miguel Villanueva (II)
3. Montealegre, Eugene Villanueva (I)
4. Montealegre, Jessica Villanueva (I)

ERNESTINA QUIJANO SALCEDO +m. (?) BAUTISTA LINE

1. Bautista, Bremel Salcedo (I)
2. Bautista, Pipon Salcedo (I)

HECTOR ABRAHAM QUIJANO Sr. +m JOSEFINA MANALANG LINE

1. Ulpindo, Cielo Quijano (I)
2. Quijano, Hector Manalang Jr. (II)
3. Quijano, Mario Manalang (I)
4. Nagaoka, Rebecca Quijano (I)
5. Quijano, Julio Manalang (II)
6. Kalaw, Joselyn Quijano (I)
7. Quijano, José Manalang (VI)
8. Quijano, Ricardo Manalang (II)
9. Quijano, Felipe Manalang (I)
10. Quijano, Antonio Manalang (XI)

FIFTH GENERATION: OF PEDRO ARANA VILLANUEVA AND QUITERIA MABIHIS VILLANUEVA LINE

PAZ PATO VILLANUEVA SR. +m CASIANO GUINTO LINE

1. Guinto, Chito Villanueva (I)
2. Santiago, Delia Guinto (I)
3. Villabroza, Paz Guinto Jr. (II)
4. Enverga, Bessie Guinto (I)
5. Guinto, Clarence Villanueva (I)
6. Guinto, Rey Villanueva (I)
7. Marchan, Joy Guinto (I)
8. Velarde, Gigie Guinto (I)

CELIA PATO VILLANUEVA +m DOMINADOR ALBARICO LINE

1. Albarico, Edbert Villanueva (I)
2. Sedilla, Julie Albarico (I)
3. Albarico, Dennis Villanueva (I)
4. Albarico, Cesar Villanueva (I)

JOSEFINA VILLANUEVA SANTOS +m DORITO TUAÑO LINE

1. Tuaño, José Santos (VI)

ERLINDA VILLANUEVA SANTOS +m ROLANDO DURIA LINE

1. Duria, Paul Santos (I)
2. Duria, Dinnes Santos (I)
3. Boyer, Marie Jane Santos (I)

MARGARITA VILLANUEVA DE LEJOS +m ANASTACIO BUENCONSEJO SR. LINE

1. Bobis, Emma Buenconsejo (II)
2. Buenconsejo, Edgar de Lejos (II)
3. Lao, Edna Buenconsejo (I)
4. Buenconsejo, Anastacio de Lejos Jr. (I)
5. Bonganay, Anita Buenconsejo (I)
6. Buenconsejo, Noel de Lejos (I)

MURIEL VILLANUEVA DE LEJOS +m. SANTIAGO ESTEVEZ RIOSA SR. LINE

1. Villar, Evelyn Riosa (I)
2. Riosa, Santiago de Lejos Jr. (II)

SOFIA REMEDIOS DE LOS ANGELES DE LEJOS +m. ROLANDO PLETA LINE

1. Hall, Judy Pleta (I)
2. Smith, Mejilla Pleta (I)
3. Herrera, Grace Pleta (III)
4. Pleta, Joan de Lejos (I)

ELVIRA VILLANUEVA +m. DR. REY GARCIA LINE

1. Tuazon, Maria Rae Cynthia Garcia (I)
2. Garcia, Peter Raymond Villanueva (I)

ANTONIO VILLANUEVA +m. ELSA BUENAVENTURA LINE

1. Villanueva, Marcela Buenaventura (I)
2. Villanueva, Fatima Buenaventura (I)

CONCHITA BOBIS VILLANUEVA +m. CARLOS JAYMALIN LINE

1. Jaymalin, Glen Villanueva (I)
2. Jaymalin, Cynthia Villanueva (II)
3. Jaymalin, Michael Villanueva (I)

EDUARDO BOBIS VILLANUEVA Sr. +m. EDITHA SULO LINE

1. Villanueva, Joseph Sulo (I)
2. Villanueva, Christine Sulo (I)
3. Villanueva, Eden Sulo (I)
4. Villanueva, Eduardo Jr. Sulo (II)
5. Villanueva, Janet Sulo (I)
6. Villanueva, Jordan Sulo (I)
7. Villanueva, Carla Sulo (I)
8. Villanueva, Jonathan Sulo (I)

JOSÉ BOBIS VILLANUEVA +m. EVELYN GREGORIO LINE

1. Villanueva, Jovencion José Gregorio (I)
2. Villanueva, Annielou Gregorio (I)
3. Villanueva, Errol Aldrin Gregorio (I)
4. Lianco, Jonelyn, Villanueva (I)

PEDRO BOBIS VILLANUEVA +m. ELUMINADA BAZAR LINE

1. Villanueva, Ramil Bazar (I)
2. Evangelista, Pamela Villanueva (I)
3. Camu, Mae Villanueva (I)
4. Sikat, Ruby Ann Villanueva (I)

TERESA BOBIS VILLANUEVA +m. PORFERIO PATIAG LINE

1. Patiag, Michele Villanueva (I)
2. Patiag, Dennis Villanueva (II)
3. Patiag, Shiela Villanueva (I)
4. Patiag, Christian Villanueva (I)

NATIVIDAD BOBIS VILLANUEVA +m. EDISON PINGOL Sr. LINE

1. Pingol, Hazel Villanueva (I)
2. Pingol, Edison Jr. Villanueva (I)
3. Pingol, Amor Villanueva (I)
4. Pingol, Eric Villanueva (II)

FE NANCY BOBIS VILLANUEVA +m. AMOR GUMABAO LINE

1. Gumabao, Paulo Villanueva (I)

ROSEMARIE JOY VILLANUEVA +m. ZOILO MORAN LINE

1. Moran, Karen Villanueva (I)
2. Moran, Katrina Joy Villanueva (I)
3. Moran, Kaye Ann Villanueva (I)

MARIA LETICIA PATRICIA VILLANUEVA RIOS +m. CHARLES WILLIAM WOOD JR. LINE

1. Wood, Desyl Angela Christina Uilani Rios (I)
2. Wood, Carla Maria Jessica Rios (I)

JUANITO SALVADOR VILLANUEVA RIOS +m. ESTER FENIX LINE

1. Molato, Maria Cristina Rios (I)
2. Rios, Juan Salvador Fenix (I)
3. Rios, Maria Ester Fenix (I)
4. Rios, Craig Fenix (I)
5. Rios, Daryl Fenix (I)

EMMA VICTORIA RIOS PALOMAR + m. RICARDO DE HITTA DIÑO LINE

1. Diño, Jose Ricardo Palomar (I)
2. Boekelmann, Michaela Diño (I)
3. Diño, Max Palomar (I)

CARLOS MANUEL VILLANUEVA RIOS Sr. +m. EMMA PERALTA LINE

1. Rios, Carlos Manuel Peralta Jr. (II)
2. Anibale, Karina Rios (I)

MARIA TERESA CONCEPCION VILLANUEVA RIOS +m. DR. RESURRECION GREGORIO BRIMBUELA KARE LINE

1. Kare, Dr. Ramon Paulo Rios (I)
2. Kare, Rex Eryl Rios (I)
3. Kare, Maria Theresa Rios (I)

JAIME MIGUEL VILLANUEVA RIOS +m. AMELIA FRAGANTE LINE

1. Rios, Luis Miguel Fragante (I)
2. Arcinue, Monica Fragante (I)
3. Rios, Marian Fragante (I)

ANGELA VILLANUEVA RIOS JR. +m. TONY MING YEE HOWE LINE

1. Howe, Jonathan Tu Wah Rios (I)
2. Nye, Katrina Tu Hsiu Rios (I)
3. Howe, Jeoffrey Tu Chin Rios (I)

ANDRES VILLANUEVA RIOS +m. CORAZON MOLINA Sr. LINE

1. Rios, Corazon Molina (I)
2. Rios, Bianca Molina (I)

NO AVAILABLE INFORMATION REGARDING THE FIFTH GENERATION OF ADRIANO MIRASOL SR. LINE.

www.ingramcontent.com/pod-product-compliance
Lightning Source LLC
Chambersburg PA
CBHW081420230426
43668CB00016B/2303